D0710223

Contents

Preface

The Canada-U.S. Free Trade Agreement is the most important bilateral trade agreement ever signed by Canada and the United States. If adopted by the United States Congress and the Canadian Parliament, it will have a profound impact on the economies of both countries and the bilateral trading relationship.

Debra P. Steger, with the assistance of her colleagues at Fraser & Beatty: Colin H.H. McNairn, John F. Blakney and Richard H. Kesler, has prepared this comprehensive and timely Guide to the Canada-U.S. Free Trade Agreement. This Guide provides a thorough and concise summary of the key features of the Agreement, describes their genesis and outlines their impact on existing laws and practices. Political uncertainties remain concerning the implementation of this Agreement in both countries. The Guide includes chapters on implementation and the Omnibus Trade Bill currently before Congress.

Debra Steger practices law with Fraser & Beatty in Ottawa, specializing in the areas of international trade and competition law and policy. She is an author, lecturer and frequent commentator on Canadian and U.S. trade laws and the Canada-U.S. Free Trade Agreement. Colin McNairn is a partner with Fraser & Beatty in Toronto and Head of the Research Department of the firm. Formerly a professor of law at the University of Toronto and author of several legal publications, he has expertise in many areas, including financial institutions, investment, constitutional and immigration law.

John Blakney practices with Fraser & Beatty in Ottawa in the areas of communications, competition, computer and transportation law and policy. Formerly with the federal government, he has an extensive background in these federal regulatory areas. Rick Kesler practices tax law with Fraser & Beatty in Toronto. Formerly with the federal government, he has expertise in the areas of federal sales tax law and policy as well as customs and tariffs.

The author wishes to extend her appreciation to her colleagues, Colin McNairn, John Blakney and Rick Kesler, for their contributions to this Guide. Special thanks go to Lawson A.W. Hunter, Q.C. for his encouragement and comments on the text. Judith Fisher and John Gillespie of Fraser & Beatty, Toronto, also assisted in promoting and reviewing this Guide. My gratitude goes to Donna MacWilliam who tirelessly typed numerous drafts of this document. Joel Saltsman, Senior Legal Editor at Carswell Legal Publications, deserves special mention for his enthusiastic efforts in organizing the publication of this Guide.

Publisher's Note

The international trade field has its own distinctive vocabulary which has found its way into the Canada-U.S. Free Trade Agreement and all the writing about it. Even specialists are sometimes lost in the maze of technical terms and acronyms used in trade negotiations and international trade agreements, such as the General Agreement on Tariffs and Trade.

To make this Guide easy to understand for the average reader and the expert alike, we have, therefore, included a revised version of the detailed glossary recently published by the Canadian government.

There is also a thorough index which will lead you directly to the topic you want. Finally, we have added a directory of those government offices across the country where you can obtain copies of the Canada-U.S. Free Trade Agreement and background documents free of charge.

1

Introduction and Overview

On January 2, 1988, Prime Minister Brian Mulroney and President Ronald Reagan signed the Canada-United States Free Trade Agreement ("FTA"). The FTA is to come into effect on January 1, 1989. Its provisions are not yet in force in either country and, indeed, many aspects of the FTA will be phased in over the ten-year transition period. In many respects, the FTA is a forward-looking, evolutionary document. It will change the face of North America, but not overnight.

Some of the changes, for example, certain tariff reductions, will take effect as soon as the FTA is implemented. In other areas, such as services and investment, existing laws and practices will be maintained but new obligations and rights will coexist with them in future.

The FTA is a classic, comprehensive free trade area agreement and qualifies easily under Article XXIV of the General Agreement on Tariffs and Trade (the "GATT"). Article XXIV permits countries that have agreed to eliminate duties and other restrictive regulations of commerce on "substantially all the trade" between them to treat each other differently than they treat all other countries.

In the FTA, Canada and the United States have expressly affirmed and strengthened their existing GATT obligations, rights and commitments and agreed to cooperate further in the Uruguay Round of multilateral trade negotiations. In addition, the two countries have cleared new paths in areas not previously covered by the GATT including trade in services and investment. Although the measures agreed to by Canada and the United States in these new areas are cautious and modest, they set the stage for the development of workable new international rules in the Uruguay Round.

Under the FTA, new channels for government-to-government communication and consultation as well as bilateral mechanisms for dispute settlement will be established. These mechanisms are a significant improvement over the existing Canadian and U.S. trade laws, the GATT, the Tokyo Round Codes, and other free trade area agreements in the world. By creating a unique, formal, bilateral consultative and dispute resolution mechanism, Canada and the United States should be able to avoid and resolve major trade disputes more quickly and effectively than before.

The objectives of the FTA are:

1. to eliminate barriers to trade in goods and services between Canada and the United States;
2. to facilitate conditions of fair competition within the free trade area;
3. to liberalize conditions for investment within North America;
4. to establish effective procedures for the joint administration of the FTA and the resolution of bilateral trade disputes; and
5. to lay the foundation for future bilateral and multilateral cooperation.

In fulfilling these objectives, the FTA is extremely comprehensive in scope. It provides for the elimination of tariffs and non-tariff barriers to trade in goods and the liberalization of trade in other areas by reducing restrictions on trade in services, financial services, investment and entry of business persons into each other's territory.

.One of the keystones of the GATT, the principle of national treatment, has become the fundamental guiding principle of the FTA. With the successive rounds of tariff reductions in the GATT, there has been a proliferation of internal domestic measures taken by countries to restrict the flow of foreign goods. The national treatment rule in the GATT provides that goods imported into a member country must receive treatment under all laws, regulations, policies, or other practices of the importing country equivalent to the treatment accorded domestically-produced, directly competitive goods. This GATT principle has been affirmed in the FTA with respect to bilateral trade in goods and has been expanded to govern future regulatory developments in new areas, such as trade in services and investment. The principle of national treatment will apply to future regulations, measures or practices of the Canadian and U.S. federal governments as well as the provincial, state and local governments.

Adoption of the principle of national treatment in the areas of services and investment does not mean that Canada must regulate certain areas of services, such as telecommunications, in exactly the same manner as the United States. What it does mean is that Canada, in regulating a services industry, must not establish new laws, policies or practices that would discriminate against services provided by U.S. firms or act as disguised barriers to trade. The national treatment obligation in these new areas is, generally speaking, forward looking – that is, it does not apply to existing regulatory measures or practices except those specifically mentioned in the FTA. A special obligation is placed by the FTA on provincial and state governments to accord national treatment in future to goods, services or investment originating in the other member country.

The FTA will have an impact on almost every area of private sector activity in North America. The immediate impact on the production plans of most businesses will flow from the tariff reductions and rules of origin. However, the FTA also establishes new rules for businesses operating or investing in Canada or the United States. It sets the stage for future liberalization of trade in many areas, but it is also a cautious, realistic agreement because both countries recognized that there were costs to be incurred in moving too far, too fast. For this reason, the FTA mandates change in some areas, establishes new principles for federal and sub-national governments to follow when devising new policies in future, and provides for further elaboration of international rules in several areas where the two countries could not agree to do more at this time. In the FTA, Canada and the United States have attempted to resolve many long-standing bilateral irritants as well as to establish new trade liberalizing rules for the future.

The FTA creates an economic blueprint for future trade relations between Canada and the United States that will change the climate for business. It is detailed, complex and contains many exceptions to deal with industrial realities and political sensitivities on both sides of the border. It is an extremely important commercial agreement, one that should be understood by businesses and consumers in both Canada and the United States. This book is an attempt to describe clearly and concisely the essence of the FTA, and to interpret its importance for business people and consumers in both countries.

2

Trade In Goods

The key feature of the FTA is the elimination of duties and certain other restrictions on substantially all the trade in goods between Canada and the United States. Both countries will retain their respective tariff schedules and other border measures for all goods imported from third countries as well as those not meeting the FTA rules of origin. The removal of bilateral customs tariffs will not occur all at once. Instead, bilateral tariffs, tariff-related measures and other restrictive measures applied at the border will be phased out over a ten-year transition period beginning January 1, 1989. After the FTA comes into effect, no existing tariff rate on goods flowing in bilateral trade may be increased unless specifically permitted in the FTA. For example, either country may increase a duty as a temporary emergency action to alleviate adjustment difficulties experienced by a domestic industry which is being seriously injured as a result of a sudden increase in imports flowing from the FTA tariff reductions.

Only bilateral tariffs on goods meeting the FTA rules of origin will be phased out. Any goods not having the required North American content will be subject to the Most-Favoured-Nation tariff in effect in the importing country. Any goods currently free of duty will remain duty free. Bilateral tariff reductions will take place in three equal stages. All dutiable products have been classified into one of three categories. Those designated in Category A will be declared duty free as of January 1, 1989. Those in Category B will have their existing tariffs phased out at a rate of 20 per cent per year commencing January 1, 1989. These products will be duty free by January 1, 1993. Those in Category C will have their tariffs phased out at a rate of 10 per cent per year also beginning January 1, 1989. Products in Category C will be duty free by January 1, 1998.

The following products are included in Category A and will be declared duty free as of January 1, 1989:

computers and equipment	some pork
some unprocessed fish	fur and fur garments
leather	whiskey
yeast	animal feeds
unwrought aluminum	ferro alloys
vending machines and parts	needles
airbrakes for railroad cars	skis
skates	warranty repairs
some paper-making machinery	motorcycles

The following products are included in Category B and will be subject to tariff reductions of 20 per cent per year over five years:

subway cars	chemicals including resin
printed matter	(excluding drugs and
paper and paper products	cosmetics)
paints	furniture
explosives	hardwood plywood
aftermarket auto parts	most machinery

The following products are classified in Category C and will be subject to tariff reductions of 10 per cent per year, commencing January 1, 1989:

most agricultural products	steel
textiles and apparel	applicances
softwood plywood	pleasure craft
railcars	tires

Tariffs on agricultural products will be phased out over 10 years, but there is a special 20-year tariff "snapback" provision for fresh fruit and vegetables. Under the latter provision, a temporary duty may be applied on fresh fruits or vegetables where the import price falls below a specified support price threshold and the planted acreage for that product in the importing country remains constant or has declined over the previous five years.

Canada and the United States were to conform to a new system of classifying products for tariff purposes, the International Convention on the Harmonized Commodity Description and Coding System (the "H.S."), on January 1, 1988. The H.S. was approved by the Customs Co-operation Council, an international body responsible for harmonizing customs procedures, in 1983. Canada signed the Convention on December 10, 1986 and implemented the H.S. on January 1, 1988. The United States has not adopted the H.S. as yet, but is expected to implement it as part of an Omnibus Trade Bill in 1988. Under the H.S., products are classified on the basis of what they are or what they are made of.

Canada implemented the H.S. in amendments to the Customs Tariff (Bill C-87). It was intended that Canadian tariff rates for specific products would remain at the same levels as they were under the former Customs Tariff. However, as a result of changing to a system with infinitely more tariff headings, some products may be dutiable at a different rate than before. The H.S. has been used in the FTA to provide the basis for tariff classification of goods on which the tariff reductions and rules of origin will be applied.

Bilateral tariff reductions on particular goods may be accelerated where both countries agree. To implement this provision, it is likely that both countries will adopt mechanisms to enable individual businesses or industries to request that the duty on goods they manufacture or import be reduced earlier than designated in the FTA.

The emergency action provisions of the FTA may be invoked by either country to reinstate a previous tariff level where increased imports from the other country cause or threaten to cause serious injury to a domestic industry. The imposition of such a measure, however, may be taken only once for a particular product and only in the transition period (i.e., until 1998).

Special provisions deal with certain products and equipment. Tariff reductions on certain specialty steel products that are currently subject to U.S. section 201 measures will not commence until October 1, 1989. Bilateral tariffs on large telephone switching equipment will be phased out in three annual stages by January 1, 1991. As a final point of interest, Canada has undertaken to continue to provide a waiver on customs duties on certain machinery and equipment considered "not available" from Canadian suppliers and certain repair and replacement parts originating in the United States.

RULES OF ORIGIN

An important feature of any free trade area agreement is its rules of origin. Only dutiable goods meeting the rules of origin established in the FTA will be accorded preferential tariff treatment. In a free trade area, member countries retain their own tariff schedules and customs measures with respect to non-member countries. As a result, there is an incentive for foreign exporters to ship products originating in a third country through the member country with the lower tariff rate and then on into the other member country duty free. For this reason, it is important that there be appropriate rules of origin to prevent such deflections of trade.

Rules of origin are used to determine in what circumstances a product may be said to originate in either Canada or the United States and, therefore, to be entitled to preferential tariff treatment under the FTA. Without such rules of origin, it would be a simple matter, for example, for a foreign company to export goods to the United States, pay the U.S. duty, and then arrange for the goods to be shipped to Canada duty free, thereby avoiding the Canadian duty that would otherwise have been payable had the goods been exported directly. The purpose of the FTA rules of origin is to ensure that the benefits of the free trade agreement are accorded only to products with substantial North American content.

In their simplest terms, the FTA rules of origin require that goods traded bilaterally must "originate" in either Canada or the United States or both to receive preferential tariff treatment. As a general principle, goods will be considered to originate in either country or both where they are wholly produced or obtained in either Canada or the United States or both, or where they have been sufficiently changed in either country so as to meet the FTA rules of origin tests. Goods "wholly obtained or produced" in either country will include goods such as minerals extracted in the territory of either country, products harvested in the territory of either country, live animals or fish raised in the territory of either country, waste or scrap derived from manufacturing and collected from the territory of either country, and goods produced in the territory of either country exclusively from the goods mentioned above. In addition, goods will be considered to originate in either country or both if they have been changed so as to be subject to a specified change in their tariff classification and, in some cases, to meet certain minimum levels of processing or assembly in either country or both.

There is no general rule of origin applicable to all products. The FTA contains precise rules, delineated by tariff heading, which specify the necessary change required for a particular good to qualify for preferential tariff treatment under the FTA. Certain specified goods, usually those which have undergone an assembly process, are required to meet a special FTA "value standard." For specified goods, the value of materials originating in the territory of either country or both plus the direct cost of manufacturing or processing performed in either country or both must constitute not less than 50 per cent of the value of the goods exported to the other country. The FTA rules of origin define such terms as "direct cost" of processing and assembling, and provide guidelines as to how to calculate the value of materials and goods. The purpose for the FTA value standard and the change of tariff heading rule is to ensure that the benefits of preferential tariff treatment will accrue only to goods with substantial Canadian and/or U.S content.

Even where these rules of origin are met, goods subsequently further processed or assembled in a third country and imported back into Canada or the United States will not qualify for preferential FTA treatment. This provision has been specifically designed to prevent goods processed further in Mexico and returned to the United States at reduced tariff rates under the U.S. tariff 807 provision from qualifying for preferential FTA tariff treatment.

In certain cases, offshore goods may qualify for preferential treatment under the FTA where they have been sufficiently changed in either Canada or the U.S. or both to be classified differently from the raw materials or components from which they were made. In other cases, goods will need to incur a certain percentage of direct processing or manufacturing cost in either or both member countries. Therefore, goods imported in bulk and simply repackaged and labelled in either country or parts imported and merely assembled in one member country would not qualify for preferential FTA treatment. On the other hand, a product that was manufactured largely in Canada and incorporated only some imported components in most instances would qualify. The rules of origin under the FTA are extremely detailed and should be consulted directly when assessing the dutiable status of a particular product.

Since the rules of origin will play such a significant role in determining the dutiable status of imported goods and materials, the FTA has incorporated a general "anti-avoidance" provision which provides that where the facts indicate that goods have undergone processing or assembly merely to circumvent the rules of origin, such goods will not qualify as originating in either country or both and, hence, will not be entitled to preferential tariff treatment.

Accessories, spare parts and tools which form part of the standard equipment of machinery or vehicles will be deemed to have the same origin as the machinery or vehicles of which they are a part, provided that the quantities and values of such parts and accessories are customary for that equipment.

Unique tariff-rate quota arrangements have been proposed for Canadian exports to the United States of apparel and textiles made from offshore fabrics as well as U.S. exports to Canada of apparel made from offshore fabrics. Apparel made wholly from Canadian or U.S. fabrics will qualify for preferential FTA treatment into the United States. For the Canadian apparel industry, a tariff-rate quota arrangement will be established such that apparel made in Canada from offshore fabrics will receive preferential FTA treatment into the United States up to a level of 50 million square yards annually for non-woolen apparel and 6 million square yards annually for woolen apparel. The corresponding levels for apparel exported to Canada from the United States will be 10.5 million square yards for non-woolen apparel and 1.1 million square yards for woolen apparel. Above the specified levels, apparel made from offshore fabrics will be liable to pay duty at the Most-Favoured-Nation rates, however, duty drawbacks will be available.

For the textile industry, fabrics made in Canada from offshore yarns and exported to the United States will receive preferential FTA treatment up to an annual level of 30 million square yards. The U.S. textile industry will not receive the same benefit. The apparel and textile rules will be reviewed within two years after the FTA comes into effect, and unless renewed, will expire by the end of 1992.

DUTY WAIVERS AND REMISSIONS

Canadian customs law permits duties on certain imported goods to be refunded to specific firms on condition that these firms meet certain performance requirements related to production, exports or employment. For example, Canadian shirt manufacturers are entitled to a refund of the duty on certain shirts, which they import from Hong

Kong, provided they manufacture one shirt in Canada for every imported shirt. This practice is known as duty waivers or remissions. The FTA provides that neither country may, after the later of June 30, 1988 or the date the FTA is approved by the U.S. Congress, introduce or expand any existing duty waiver or remission program where such waiver is conditional upon the fulfillment of any trade-related performance requirement. Except for the automotive industry (which is subject to its own set of rules), existing duty waiver and remission programs linked to performance requirements are to be eliminated by 1998.

In certain cases, duty waivers or remissions are granted on an unconditional basis. Waivers or remissions of this nature are usually granted to a specific company or industry for a limited period of time. These waiver and remission programs will be allowed to continue except that where such a program has an adverse impact on the commercial interests of a person or a firm in the other country, that country may complain, and the country providing the waiver will be required to either cease granting it or make it available to all importers.

DUTY DRAWBACKS

Both Canada and the United States have programs providing for the refund of customs duties paid on imported goods that are subsequently exported or are incorporated into goods that are subsequently exported. Duty drawbacks are provided so as not to discourage assembly and manufacturing in either Canada or the United States and to ensure that goods ultimately destined for export and dutiable in the country of final destination are not subject to duty twice.

With the elimination of tariffs between Canada and the U.S., the need for duty drawbacks on bilateral trade will be eliminated and these programs will end by January 1, 1994. The rules of origin are designed to ensure that only goods or materials with sufficient North American content will be given preferential tariff treatment under the FTA. The drawbacks allowed for goods that simply enter Canada or the United States under bond for transshipment in the same condition to the other country will be allowed to continue. For the purpose of this exception, testing, cleaning, repacking or inspecting the goods, preserving them in their same condition, or other similar processing will not be considered as a process that would change the condition of the goods.

Duty drawbacks will continue to be available for imported citrus products as well as for imported fabrics used in making apparel subsequently exported to the other country above the permissible tariff-rate quota levels established in the FTA. Drawbacks will continue for these products as they will be subject to the Most-Favoured-Nation tariff when exported to the other country.

IMPORT AND EXPORT RESTRICTIONS

Both countries have agreed that they will only establish or maintain import or export quantitative restrictions (or quotas) that are in accordance with the GATT. The GATT permits the establishment of quantitative restrictions for the purposes of domestic agricultural and fisheries support programs, health and safety reasons, or serious balance of payments difficulties. Export restrictions in the form of quantitative restrictions or export licensing requirements are permitted under the GATT to relieve critical shortages of products, conserve exhaustible natural resources, or ensure essential quantities of materials required by a domestic processing industry as part of a governmental stabilization program.

Where such measures are taken by either Canada or the United States in future, the FTA provides that the proportion of the good exported to the other country must not be reduced relative to the total domestic supply of the good as compared with the proportion exported prior to the imposition of the export restriction. Any new export restriction must not be designed to disrupt normal channels of supply or proportions among particular restricted goods. The use of export licences, fees, taxes or other charges by governments as a disguised restriction to charge higher prices for export sales than for domestic sales is prohibited.

The FTA affirms the GATT prohibitions on certain forms of quantitative restrictions, including minimum export-price or import-price requirements. Certain existing quantitative restrictions will be eliminated. Among these will be the Canadian embargos on used automobiles and used aircraft, and the U.S. embargo on lottery materials. Canada will retain its right to control log exports to the United States, while the United States will retain its shipping restrictions under the *Jones Act*. The provincial restrictions on exports of unprocessed fish currently in effect in Quebec, Nova Scotia, New Brunswick, Prince Edward Island and Newfoundland will be exempt from the FTA. Restrictions on exports of unprocessed salmon and herring from British Columbia are currently the subject of a GATT panel report, and are not mentioned in the FTA. Both countries have agreed to retain their rights and obligations under the GATT, including their rights to challenge a non-conforming measure, with respect to existing fish processing and beer restrictions.

Although neither Canada nor the United States applies taxes on exports as a matter of policy, export taxes are not specifically prohibited in the GATT. The FTA prohibits the imposition of an export tax or charge on goods unless the same tax is applied on goods consumed domestically. The export tax charged by the Canadian government on exports of softwood products to the United States, as a result of the 1986 Softwood Lumber Memorandum of Understanding, is maintained under the FTA until such time as provincial government replacement measures are in effect.

Also, the U.S. customs user fee, imposed in 1987 and the subject of a GATT challenge by Canada, will be phased out by January 1, 1994. The United States applies a customs user fee calculated as a percentage of the value of each import transaction (currently 0.17 per cent), and exporters must pay this additional charge even on products that are free of duty. Both countries are prohibited in future from establishing new customs user fees on goods meeting the FTA rules of origin.

CUSTOMS PROCEDURES

Under the FTA, customs procedures are to be simplified. Also, cooperation between Canadian and U.S. customs authorities is to be enhanced. Importers will be required to provide written declarations, based on exporters' written certifications, that goods imported from the other country meet the FTA rules of origin. Upon request, an importer will be required to provide customs officials in the importing country with proof of the exporter's written certification of the origin of the goods. An exporter is also required, upon request, to provide written certification of the origin of goods it exports to the other country.

Canadian and U.S. customs authorities are to cooperate, in future, particularly in matters relating to administration and enforcement of customs laws, uniform application of rules of origin, collection of import and export statistics, harmonization of documents used in trade, and exchange of information.

3

Product Standards

The FTA contains measures aimed at ensuring that product standards and certification and testing procedures imposed by the federal governments do not create unnecessary barriers to Canada-U.S. trade in goods. Product standards and technical regulations are used frequently by governments for health and safety, consumer protection and environmental reasons. There are also private standardizing bodies, such as the Canadian Standards Association and the American Society for Testing and Materials, which set voluntary standards for products. Product standards and certification and testing procedures are particularly important to agricultural, food, beverage and packaging producers. Special provisions in the FTA deal with these products.

As a starting point, Canada and the United States have affirmed their respective rights and obligations under the GATT Agreement on Technical Barriers to Trade, which came into effect in 1980. The basic principle of that Agreement, as affirmed in the FTA, is that neither country is to maintain or introduce standards-related measures or procedures for product testing or certification that would create unnecessary obstacles to trade. Measures or procedures designed to protect health, safety, national security, environmental or consumer interests are deemed not to be unnecessary obstacles to trade as long as they do not operate to exclude goods of the other country where these goods would otherwise meet the permitted domestic regulatory objectives. The FTA will not require that Canadian and U.S. standards be identical, only that domestic standards and product approval procedures be applied equally to goods originating in either country.

Standards-related measures are defined broadly to include technical specifications, technical regulations, product standards, testing and certification procedures that apply to goods as well as to processes and production methods. The two countries have agreed to make their standards-related measures and product approval procedures compatible as much as possible in future in accordance with international standardization activities. For the purposes of the FTA, standards compatibility means that differing standards, technical regulations or certification systems approved by different standardizing bodies should be recognized as being technically equivalent or identical in practice. Compatibility does not necessarily mean adoption of the same standards or approval methods and procedures. Thus, for example, Canada and the United States may continue to employ different regulatory tests for chronic toxicity, such as carcinogenicity, but the two countries have agreed to move towards acceptance of each other's tests and results.

In both countries, private bodies and independent, publicly-funded agencies are responsible for the development of voluntary industry standards and testing procedures. Canada and the United States have agreed to use their best efforts to promote compatibility in standards-related measures developed or maintained by private standardizing bodies.

A foreign country's requirements for testing and approval are often of great practical importance to the introduction of products into new markets. Often only domestic testing agencies are accredited for examining and testing these new products. The result is that significant, and often unnecessary, costs and delays are sometimes incurred in introducing a product into a new market even though it has been tested extensively in the home country, and there is no substantive difference between the regulatory standards of the two countries.

In an important step, both federal governments have agreed to recognize each other's accreditation systems and will not require in future that testing facilities, inspection agencies or certification bodies be located or established within the importing country. Fees charged in either country by testing facilities, inspection agencies or certification bodies must be reasonable and are limited to the approximate cost of the services rendered.

The FTA provides for a new, formal binational notice and comment process when either federal government proposes to adopt a new regulatory standard. This process builds upon the procedures for notification and consultation under the GATT Agreement on Technical Barriers to Trade as well as domestic regulatory review procedures. In the United States, the *Administrative Procedure Act* establishes a detailed notice and comment procedure for rules made by federal agencies, such as the Environmental Protection Agency. It has also been Canadian government policy since early 1986 to require federal government departments and agencies to give advance notice of proposed regulations, to consult extensively with affected businesses and consumers in preparing regulations that pertain to them, and to "pre-publish" draft regulations for public comment prior to their becoming law.

Under the FTA, Canada and the United States have agreed to notify each other about proposed federal government standards-related measures and product approval procedures in sufficient time to give the other country an opportunity to comment or ask questions about the possible impact on bilateral trade. Prior notification is not required in special circumstances where delay might frustrate achieving an important health, safety, national security, environmental or consumer protection objective.

In addition, where feasible, each country has undertaken to notify the other of proposed provincial and state standards-related measures that may significantly affect bilateral trade, provide persons of the other country with information concerning proposed provincial and state regulations, and take steps to notify the other country of standards-related measures of major private standardizing organizations. Without directly obliging provincial or state regulators or private standardizing bodies to conform to the FTA, the two countries have established a mechanism to increase the transparency of these measures. These notification obligations on the federal governments may provide a useful means to increase awareness of provincial and state regulatory barriers to trade.

Finally, Canada and the United States have agreed to continue negotiations on regulatory compatibility of product standards, accreditation and acceptance of test data.

An effective institutional mechanism to reduce or inhibit the establishment of non-tariff barriers, such as discriminatory product standards and product approval requirements, is a necessary complement to the elimination of tariffs between Canada and the United States. Otherwise, as tariffs are eliminated on products moving between the two countries, there would be incentives for, and indeed, domestic pressures on, governments to erect non-tariff barriers to inhibit the flow of foreign goods. The product standards chapter will not require changes to existing standards-related measures or necessarily require the harmonization of Canadian and U.S. measures in future. It will, however, establish notification and consultation mechanisms that will act as a deterrent to the creation of new discriminatory standards in future.

As a result of the GATT Agreement on Technical Barriers to Trade and the considerable integration that already exists between the Canadian and U.S. economies, product standards in both countries are essentially consistent, except for a few areas such as electrical products and agricultural and food products. In Canada, a large number of provincial standards are developed in accordance with federal "model" standards, such as the National Building Code and the National Fire Code. Also, the standards developed by the Canadian General Standards Board (an arm of the federal Department of Supply and Services) are often adopted by reference in many provincial and municipal regulations. In addition, the Standards Council of Canada, an agency which reports to the federal Minister of Consumer and Corporate Affairs and promotes the development of national standards, will likely exert its influence to implement the objective of consistency in standards-related measures except in areas where there are demonstrable public policy objectives that require otherwise.

More concrete and discernable changes are likely to occur as a result of the FTA in the recognition and accreditation of testing and certification services in the two countries. With the obligation to provide for mutual recognition of federal accreditation of such services, a considerable reduction in duplicative product testing requirements is likely to occur. Businesses will be able to concentrate their testing resources in the country which provides the lowest cost testing service or in which their products are first introduced. This should reduce the costs and delays often incurred in introducing a new product into the other country.

4

Agricultural and Food Products

TARIFFS AND SUBSIDIES

Progress has been made in the FTA to liberalize bilateral agricultural trade. Canada and the United States have agreed to eliminate all agricultural tariffs within ten years. For fresh fruits and vegetables, where the import price of a particular product falls below a specified support price threshold and the planted acreage for that particular product is constant or declining, a temporary duty may be applied once per year on a national or a regional basis until 2008. In addition, the FTA will provide agricultural producers in each country with greater access to the other's markets by eliminating certain quantitative restrictions.

Canada and the United States have agreed to set an example for their other trading partners involved in the Uruguay Round of multilateral negotiations in this vital area. The commitments by the United States in the FTA are important because, since the 1950s, the United States has had a GATT waiver on import restrictions for agricultural products. In the FTA, Canada and the United States have set as their primary goal the elimination, on a global basis, of all subsidies that distort agricultural trade. Both countries have agreed to work together toward this goal in the Uruguay Round of multilateral trade negotiations.

The two countries have taken an important first step in agreeing to eliminate export subsidies on agricultural products traded between them. They have also agreed not to "dump" agricultural products into each other's markets at a price below the acquisition price by government agencies of those products plus related storage, handling or other costs. Canada has agreed to eliminate its rail transportation subsidies under the *Western Grain Transportation Act* for Canadian agricultural products shipped through West Coast ports for consumption in the United States. When considering granting an export subsidy in future on any agricultural product exported to a third country, each country is to consider the possible effects on the export interests of the other country.

The FTA provides some guidance as to what will be regarded as a prohibited export subsidy. Generally speaking, any government assistance that is conditional upon, or designed to encourage, the exportation of products is an export subsidy. The FTA adopts the Annex to the Subsidies and Countervailing Duties Code as an illustrative list of export subsidies. The list includes direct government grants contingent upon export performance; currency retention schemes or other practices that involve a bonus on exports; internal transportation charges for products destined for export on terms more favourable than for domestic shipments; government provision of services for the production of exports on terms more favourable than for domestic products or than those otherwise commercially available to the exporter; export-related tax exemptions, remissions or deferrals; and government export credit guarantees at terms better than those otherwise commercially available.

General price support or income stabilization programs available to farmers and fishermen, provision of infrastructure (e.g., transportation, storage facility) assistance and general credit guarantees are not generally regarded as export subsidies because they apply equally to the production of all agricultural products and do not distort trade flows. The majority of agricultural programs available in Canada and the United States are domestic programs and are not export subsidies. Domestic subsidies, although not prohibited in the FTA, may be subject to countervailing duty actions in either country.

SPECIFIC PRODUCTS

Fresh fruits and vegetables may receive limited exemptions from the FTA general tariff elimination provisions. During the first 20 years of the FTA, Canada and the United States may impose temporary duties on imports of fresh fruits and vegetables imported from the other country. Where the import price of a particular fresh fruit or vegetable falls below a support price threshold specified in the FTA and the planted acreage (excluding any acreage shifted out of wine or grape production) for that product in the importing country is constant or declining over the previous five years, a temporary duty may be applied on a regional or national basis. Such a temporary duty cannot exceed the current Most-Favoured-Nation ("MFN") rate or pre-FTA MFN rate, may only be applied once per year either nationally or regionally, and must be removed once the export price exceeds the support price threshold or no later than 180 days after its imposition.

QUANTITATIVE RESTRICTIONS

Canada and the United States have agreed not to maintain or introduce quantitative restrictions on imports of meat from the other country. When one country imposes meat import quotas on a third country, the other must cooperate to prevent the third country from bypassing these restrictions.

Canada has agreed to eliminate its import restrictions on imports of U.S. grain products, such as wheat, oats and barley and related products, once the level of government support in the United States for any of those grain products has been determined to be equal to or less than the level of government support for the same grains in Canada, subject to compliance with product standards and proof-of-end-use controls. A detailed annex specifies the formulae to be used to calculate the level of government support for grain production in each country. Federal as well as state and provincial programs providing direct or indirect subsidies are to be included in this calculation. The relevant calculations in some cases will be performed by a Working Group, made up of three representatives from each country, within a specific time frame and subject to binding arbitration in the event of a disagreement. This support payment annex should prove to be an important precedent in developing comparative tests of subsidy levels for other agricultural products as well as for the GATT Uruguay Round negotiations on agricultural subsidies.

In Canada, poultry and eggs are regulated by national and provincial marketing boards, which set national and provincial product quotas and restrict imports. These programs were established partly to protect Canadian primary producers of poultry and eggs from foreign competition. It was felt that the economies of scale that U.S. poultry and egg· producers, in particular, enjoy from production facilities designed to serve larger and more populous U.S. markets could easily enable U.S. producers to capture the Canadian market at prices Canadians could not match.

These marketing boards are untouched by the FTA with the exception of two minor changes. First, the level of "global import quota" on poultry and eggs available to be filled by U.S. or other foreign exports will be set at varying specific percentages of the current year's national production quota, in the case of chickens and turkeys, and on the previous year's actual production in the case of eggs. Second, a variety of higher value-added poultry and egg products will be excluded from the definition of chicken and turkey products in the application of Canadian import quotas. The FTA will continue to permit import restrictions on popular low-end processed products (such as breaded chicken fingers and chicken nuggets), but will discourage Canadian poultry producers and processors from seeking import restrictions on newer high-margin processed products (such as chicken kiev or frozen turkey TV dinners).

For its part, the United States has agreed to eliminate import quotas and fees on Canadian goods containing 10 per cent or less sugar by dry weight for the purposes of restricting the sugar content of such goods.

PRODUCT STANDARDS

Over the years, there have been a large number of complaints on both sides of the border that technical health, safety and grading regulations, their interpretation by officials, and inspection practices have been used as effective barriers to trade. *Ad hoc* regulatory actions, particularly with respect to perishable agricultural products where secure and timely supplies are critical, can often be effective as non-tariff barriers. To reduce the potential for such barriers in the future, Canada and the United States have agreed to new principles, institutional arrangements and a work program for the harmonization of technical regulations and product standards for agricultural, food, beverage and certain related products.

The two countries have agreed to seek an "open border policy" in the trade of agricultural and food products and to be guided by the following principles in future:

- harmonization or equivalency of respective technical requirements and inspection procedures;
- application of import or quarantine restrictions only on the basis of regional, and not national, distribution of diseases or pests in the exporting country where they are actually distributed regionally;
- establishment of equivalent accreditation procedures for inspection systems and inspectors;
- establishment of reciprocal training programs and, where appropriate, cross-utilization of inspection personnel;
- common data and confirmation requirements for the approval of new products and processes.

Canada and the United States have also agreed to work towards the elimination of technical regulations and product standards that are arbitrary, unjustified or disguised restrictions on bilateral trade; to exchange information about technical regulations, standards and testing; and to notify and consult with each other during the development of new regulations and product standards that may affect bilateral trade in agricultural or related goods.

The special agreement on technical standards for agricultural and food products will be implemented through a number of product-specific Working Groups, which will report to a joint monitoring committee. It in turn, will report to the Canadian Minister of Agriculture and the U.S. Secretary of Agriculture. In particular, Working Groups will be established for:

- Animal Health
- Plant Health, Seeds and Fertilizers
- Meat and Poultry Inspection
- Dairy, Fruit, Vegetable and Egg Inspection
- Veterinary Drugs and Feeds
- Food, Beverage, and Colour Additives and Unavoidable Contaminants
- Pesticides
- Packaging and Labelling

No deadlines have been attached to achieving any of these specific goals in the FTA. The principal incentives towards achievement of them would appear to be the obligation on the part of both countries to report on progress on a regular basis and the responsibility of the joint monitoring committee to report on progress, or the lack of it, to the Canada-U.S. Trade Commission.

5

Automotive Trade

The automotive industry is the largest employer in Canada and represents by far the greatest percentage of bilateral trade in manufactured goods. The Agreement Concerning Automotive Products Between the Government of the United States and the Government of Canada (the "Auto Pact") has, since 1965, provided duty-free access to each other's markets.

However, all was not secure with the Auto Pact. The U.S. auto parts and automobile manufacturers, concerned about increasing competition from off-shore manufacturers, were threatening to launch a countervailing duty action against Canadian duty remission and incentive programs. The U.S. dissatisfaction was intense and some observers contemplated that within a few years the United States might serve notice to terminate the Auto Pact.

The FTA has preserved the Canadian duty remission programs for manufacturers that qualify under the Auto Pact. Under the FTA, all tariffs between Canada and the United States on vehicles and auto parts will be phased out over 10 years. The elimination of tariffs on automotive products will mean that off-shore automobile manufacturers with plants in Canada or the United States, who did not qualify under the Auto Pact, will be able to source parts from all over North America. The Most-Favoured-Nation tariff will remain in place on vehicles and auto parts imported from third countries.

All automobile producers that qualify under the Auto Pact will continue to be able to import vehicles and parts duty free into Canada from anywhere in the world as long as they maintain the Auto Pact safeguards. The list of qualified producers under the Auto Pact is long and includes the "big three" automobile manufacturers as well as over 100 others, including Volvo Canada Ltd., Navistar International Corporation Canada, American Motors (Canada) Ltd., Bricklin Canada Ltd. and Bombardier Inc. The "big three" North American manufacturers: Chrysler, Ford and General Motors currently save approximately $300 million annually from the duty remission provisions of the Auto Pact.

A new, stricter rule of origin will apply to all vehicles traded between Canada and the United States. To qualify for duty free treatment, 50 per cent of the direct production costs of any vehicle traded will have to be incurred in Canada or the United States or both. Canadian parts manufacturers, however, are lobbying for a 60 per cent direct cost of processing rule of origin.

The purpose of the automotive chapter of the FTA is to benefit and promote employment and production of automobiles and auto parts in Canada and the United States. The effect of the measures agreed to in the FTA will be to reduce Canadian duty remission incentive programs for off-shore manufacturers, particularly those conditioned upon exports to the United States. With the existing overcapacity and predicted decline in industry sales over the next few years, the intent of the FTA is to strengthen the North American automotive industry against the growing tide of imports.

Canada has agreed to eliminate its duty remission programs for a number of European and Asian auto manufacturers with plants in Canada. Both countries have agreed, furthermore, that there are to be no new qualified producers under the Auto Pact. Duty remission programs based on exports to the United States will terminate effective January 1, 1989. Other export-based duty remission programs will terminate by 1998. Duty remission programs for off-shore manufacturers that are based on Canadian value-added contained in production in Canada will expire by 1996. The companies currently benefiting from these latter programs are Honda Canada Inc., Hyundai Auto Canada Inc., Toyota Motor Manufacturing Canada Inc. and CAMI Automotive Inc.

Both countries have agreed not to introduce a new program or extend the application of an existing duty remission program, where the duty remission is based on production or performance requirements, after June 30, 1988 or the date that the FTA is approved by Congress, whichever is later.

With the exception of duty remission programs for Auto Pact producers and those explicitly agreed to be phased out over periods set out in the FTA, both countries will have the opportunity to challenge an existing duty remission program for automotive goods where it has an adverse or injurious impact on the commercial interests of a firm operating in the other country.

The Canadian government has agreed to phase out its prohibition on importation of used automobiles from the United States in five annual stages commencing on January 1, 1989. By 1994, there will be no restrictions on importation of used automobiles from the United States.

To improve the competitiveness of the North American automotive industry, the governments of Canada and the United States have agreed to create a select panel of industry representatives to assess the state of the North American industry and to suggest private and public measures that should be taken to encourage and improve North American production in future. Also, Canada and the United States have agreed to cooperate in the Uruguay Round to create new export opportunities for North American automotive products.

6

Alcoholic Beverages

In an attempt to resolve long-standing irritants to bilateral trade in alcoholic beverages, Canada and the United States have agreed to reduce some marketing and distribution restrictions to trade in wine and distilled spirits, but have agreed to maintain existing restrictions with respect to beer. Certain provincial listing, pricing and distribution practices as well as some federal blending, standards and labelling requirements for wine and distilled spirits will be changed as a result of the FTA. All other existing measures concerning the regulation of wine and distilled spirits have been grandfathered, which means that they may be maintained or be renewed, but if a measure is amended it must not be made more restrictive. With respect to beer, the two countries have agreed that existing provincial restrictions may be maintained but, in future, new policies relating to the distribution, pricing or sale of beer will have to meet the non-discriminatory national treatment standard. Furthermore, where an existing restrictive measure is amended, governments are not permitted to make it more restrictive of foreign goods.

Both Canada and the United States have expressly reserved their rights and obligations under the GATT with respect to all alcoholic beverages. This means that the United States is not prevented in future from complaining to the GATT about Canadian provincial restrictions on beer. Upon a complaint by the European Community, a GATT panel recently found Canadian provincial wine, distilled spirits and beer practices to be in violation of the GATT national treatment rule.

The FTA requires that the listing practices of provincial liquor control boards be open, fair and capable of being challenged by any applicant. In particular, the FTA will require that any listing policy not discriminate against U.S. products, that it be published and available to the public, and that there be fair, open procedures for dealing with listing applications. The listing policy of the province of British Columbia, which provides for automatic listing of locally-produced wines, may be maintained for estate wineries producing less than 30,000 gallons of wine annually.

The FTA also lays down new rules for the pricing of wine and distilled spirits. It provides for the phasing out over six years of mark-ups for wine in excess of the actual cost of service differential between U.S. products and Canadian products. All mark-ups on distilled spirits representing more than the actual cost of service differential between U.S. and Canadian products will be eliminated as of January 1, 1989. Any other discriminatory pricing measures are required to be elim-inated by provincial governments when the FTA comes into effect.

The FTA requires that provincial governments change their distribution policies and practices to treat U.S. wine and distilled spirits no less favourably than Canadian products. Special exceptions have been carved out for certain existing distribution practices for locally-produced wine in Ontario, British Columbia, and Quebec. First, any winery or distillery that sells its products in a store on its premises may restrict its sales to wines or distilled spirits produced on those premises. Second, the provinces of Ontario and British Columbia may maintain their existing restrictions allowing private wine store outlets to discriminate in favour of Ontario or British Columbia wines. Third, the province of Quebec may continue its requirement that any wine sold in grocery stores be bottled in Quebec, provided that there are government liquor stores or other outlets available for the sale of U.S. wine in Quebec.

The government of Canada is required to eliminate any of its existing regulations which provide that distilled spirits imported in bulk from the United States must be blended with Canadian spirits before being bottled. Also, Canada and the United States have agreed to reciprocally recognize the U.S. standard for bourbon whiskey and the Canadian standard for Canadian whiskey. Canada will not permit the sale of any product identified as bourbon whiskey unless it has been manufactured in the United States and complies with U.S. standards. Similarly, the United States has agreed to recognize Canadian whiskey as a distinctive product of Canada, and will not permit the sale of any product identified as Canadian whiskey unless it has been manufactured in Canada in accordance with Canadian standards.

The provisions of the FTA pertaining to wine, distilled spirits and beer will apply also to coolers and other beverages containing wine, distilled spirits or malt.

7

Energy

EXPORT AND IMPORT RESTRICTIONS

Canadian energy exports to the U.S. currently exceed $10 billion per year. Obtaining secure market access for these exports was a high priority on Canada's agenda during the free trade negotiations. Of equal importance to the United States was restraining Canada's ability, in future, to impose export restrictions, such as the restrictive export licensing requirements and the regulated two-price system for domestic and export products that had existed under the National Energy Program.

Energy goods covered by the FTA are coal and its byproducts, petroleum, natural gas, electricity, uranium, nuclear fuel and heavy water. Canada and the United States have affirmed their GATT rights and obligations with respect to restrictions on bilateral trade in these energy goods, including the GATT prohibition on minimum export-price requirements and minimum import-price requirements. Export taxes, fees or charges on energy goods are also prohibited under the FTA. The FTA does not prevent either country from limiting or prohibiting imports from the other country of energy goods originating from third countries in order to enforce import restrictions on third countries.

The provisions of the energy chapter relating to export and import restrictions parallel those provisions relating to goods generally. Both Canada and the United States may continue to impose export and import restrictions that are permitted under the GATT. These include temporary prohibitions or restrictions to prevent or relieve critical shortages of an essential product; conservation measures for exhaustible natural resources as long as there are also restrictions on domestic production or consumption; export restrictions necessary to ensure essential supplies of a product to a domestic processing industry during periods when a domestic price is held below world price as part of a government stabilization plan; and measures essential to the acquisition or distribution of products in general or local short supply.

However, where export restrictions are imposed in such circumstances, they must not reduce the proportion of the energy good exported to the other country relative to the total supply of the good as compared to the proportion exported in the most recent 36-month period. Restrictive measures such as licences, fees, taxation, and minimum price requirements cannot be used by a government to impose a higher price on exports of an energy good to the other country than that charged for the same goods for domestic consumption. Also, such restrictions cannot be used to disrupt normal channels of supply to the other country or the normal proportions among specific energy goods supplied to the other country. Where there is any inconsistency between the FTA and the Agreement on an International Energy Program ("IEP"), the provisions of the IEP are to override the provisions of the FTA.

Import or export restrictions on energy goods for national security reasons will be permitted only to the extent that they are needed to supply a military establishment, enable fulfilment of a critical defence contract, respond to a situation of armed conflict, implement national or international policies on nuclear weapons non-proliferation, or respond to direct threats of disruption in the supply of nuclear materials for defence purposes.

ELECTRICITY, OIL AND NATURAL GAS

Consistent with the FTA principles, Canada has agreed to eliminate as part of the National Energy Board's ("NEB") export licensing requirements for electrical power, the requirement to provide evidence that the export price would not result in prices in the importing country materially less than the least cost alternative for electrical power at the same location within that country. The FTA does not expressly provide for elimination of any other NEB export licensing tests. Application by the NEB of any test of that energy to be exported must be surplus to foreseeable Canadian requirements ("surplus test") and will have to be consistent with the general national treatment and proportionality rules of the FTA. In 1986, the NEB modified its methods for determining whether natural gas intended for export is surplus. Those changes reduced the burden on applicants and provided a more relaxed monitoring of natural gas supply and demand.

Canada and the United States may continue to provide existing and new incentives for oil and gas exploration, development and related activities to maintain the reserve base of these resources. This applies to the provincial and state governments as well as the federal governments. However, either country may continue to apply its countervailing duty laws against such government subsidies.

URANIUM

Canada has agreed to exempt the United States from the requirement of the Canadian Uranium Upgrading Policy that only uranium which has been further processed in Canada may be exported. The United States has agreed, in turn, to exempt Canada from its restrictions on the enrichment of foreign uranium under the *Atomic Energy Act of 1954*. This ends a long regulatory battle which had threatened Canadian exports of uranium to the United States. Canada currently supplies over 80 per cent of U.S. uranium requirements.

CONCLUSION

The immediate impact of the energy chapter of the FTA will not be pronounced. Some bilateral irritants have been eliminated but, as long as supplies are abundant and prices are soft, few incentives will exist for either country to impose restrictive, discriminatory import or export measures. The real test of the FTA's energy provisions will occur if governments perceive once again, as they did in the mid-1970s, that domestic supplies of energy products, such as petroleum and natural gas, are being depleted and must be conserved.

The FTA makes it clear that governments may continue in future to use import or export restrictions for legitimate conservation reasons or to assure domestic security of supply. The principal new limitations on such measures are that export taxes are prohibited and any new import or export restrictions imposed cannot have a discriminatory, non-proportional impact on the other country.

8

Government Procurement

A MODEST BEGINNING

An important Canadian objective in the negotiations was to gain greater access for Canadian suppliers to the large U.S. government procurement market. The achievements of the FTA in this respect are modest, even disappointing, but may improve over the longer term. The Canadian government projects that as a result of the FTA, Canadian suppliers will gain access to approximately $3 billion (U.S.) more in U.S. federal government contracts, while U.S. suppliers will gain access to approximately $500 million (U.S.) more federal government business in Canada.

Essentially, the FTA will subject a larger number of U.S. and Canadian federal government purchases to the rules and procedures of the Government Procurement Code by reducing the minimum value of government contracts covered by that Code to $25,000 (U.S.) or approximately $38,000 (Cdn.). The Government Procurement Code currently applies to certain types of contracts with designated federal government departments and agencies where the contract is valued at $171,000 (U.S.) or approximately $238,000 (Cdn.), or greater. Neither the Government Procurement Code nor the FTA apply to any provincial, state, or local government departments or agencies. This means that the FTA will not apply to provincially-owned public utilities.

THE GOVERNMENT PROCUREMENT CODE

The exclusions to the Government Procurement Code, and, therefore, also the FTA, are probably more extensive than the inclusions. The Code applies only to products and services incidental to the supply of products. Contracts for services, including construction, advertising or research and development, are not included. Also, the Code does not apply to military procurement of weapons or material related in any way to military security. The provisions of the Code apply, furthermore, only to federal government departments and agencies specifically listed for each country.

The Canadian list is composed essentially of departments of the government of Canada and some major federal agencies. However, Crown corporations, such as Air Canada and the Canadian Broadcasting Corporation, are not covered. The Department of Defence is included, but only for purchases involving goods of a non-military nature such as tractors, service and trade equipment, construction equipment and office equipment. The Departments of Communications and Transport are not included in the Canadian list, nor are the Fisheries and Marine Services branches of the Department of Fisheries and the Environment.

In the United States, a large number of U.S. government departments and agencies are covered by the Government Procurement Code, with the notable exception of the Departments of Transport and Energy. Certain Department of Defense non-military purchases are covered, such as vehicles, engines, industrial equipment and components, computer software and equipment, and commercial supplies. However, purchasing programs designed to aid small businesses are not included. The *Buy America Act* provisions enforced by the U.S. federal government and several state governments continue to inhibit a large number of Canadian suppliers from obtaining contracts with U.S. governments. For instance, the U.S. Department of Defense will not purchase construction or building materials from a foreign supplier if such materials are available from U.S. firms. Specific items of export interest to Canada that are not covered in the Government Procurement Code include telecommunications, heavy electrical power generation and transmission, and transportation equipment.

The Government Procurement Code requires the federal governments of Canada and the United States to provide national treatment to Code-covered products and suppliers. It also provides that technical specifications, local preference requirements, offsets or other devices must not be used by governments to create unnecessary obstacles to trade. The Code covers all tendering qualification and contracting procedures of listed government departments and agencies. With respect to the qualification of suppliers for government contracts, the basic rule is that of non-discrimination between foreign and domestic suppliers.

Under the Code, each country is required to provide all potential suppliers in the other country with equal access to pre-solicitation information and equal opportunity to compete in the pre-notification phases. All potential suppliers must also be given equal opportunity to respond to tendering and bidding requirements. Covered U.S. and Canadian federal government departments and agencies are required to make information available in advance to potential suppliers, to base their decisions on the documents tendered, to provide advance information on their rules and procedures, and to provide written reasons for their decisions in awarding contracts to specific suppliers.

The FTA would extend the application of these Government Procurement Code principles and procedures to contracts with Code-covered federal government agencies of a threshold value of $25,000 (U.S.) or greater. The FTA will not affect the enhanced market access already provided under the Canada-U.S. Defence Production Sharing Program which provides a waiver of certain U.S. *Buy America Act* provisions for specified defence suppliers and duty free access for each other's defence products.

NEW BID CHALLENGE PROCEDURE

A new feature in the FTA is that Canada and the United States have agreed to implement an independent bid challenge procedure for unsuccessful suppliers that will permit the challenge of any aspect of the procurement bidding process. It will also require timely consideration of any complaint or challenge by the government agency or department concerned, and provide for an impartial review of a challenge or complaint. An independent reviewing agency will be established to investigate complaints where a supplier feels that it has been unfairly treated, and to recommend to the two governments changes in procurement procedures in accordance with the FTA. Implementation of the bid challenge provisions will be monitored by both governments through the exchange of procurement statistics identifying procurements by government agency and department and by product.

IMPACT OF NEW SYSTEM

The extension of the application of the Government Procurement Code to a larger number of federal government purchases together with an enhanced bid challenge procedure for unsuccessful potential suppliers should result in an incremental increase in access by U.S. and Canadian suppliers to the other country's federal government procurement market.

In Canada, the Department of Supply and Services ("DSS"), which does the bulk of the federal government's purchasing of products, has a longstanding policy of restricting tender solicitation to Canadian-based firms providing that there is sufficient competition in Canada subject to the rules and procedures of the Government Procurement Code. DSS classifies potential suppliers into one of the following groups in descending order of priority:

Group 1: Canadian-based manufacturers and processors including companies that do not manufacture in Canada but are treated as such because their global product rationalization practices have led to continued Canadian production in a related product.

Group 2: Canadian-based companies acting as *bona fide* agents of foreign manufacturers where they offer suitable after-sales service.

Group 3: Other *bona fide* Canadian-based sales agents.

Group 4: Foreign-based manufacturers or agents.

Proposals or bids will generally not be solicited from other categories if an adequate number (usually 3 or more) of Group 1 suppliers exists. If not, suppliers in Group 2 will be approached and so forth until an adequate number of suppliers is found. Suppliers with a presence (not necessarily a manufacturing presence) in a depressed Canadian region also have tended to receive favourable procurement treatment in the past.

It is doubtful that these Canadian practices will survive intact with the greater pressures for transparency and national treatment and the extension of the Government Procurement Code to a wider range of federal government purchases. However, the FTA provisions concerning government procurement will not affect provincial or state government departments, or their agencies, or federal government agencies not listed in the Code.

9

Investment

EVOLUTION OF INVESTMENT POLICIES

Government policies and programs regulating foreign direct investment have often been a source of friction in Canada-U.S. relations. In the 1950s and 1960s, a period of tremendous growth, U.S. investment flowed relatively freely into Canada. As a result, by the early 1970s about three-fifths of the Canadian manufacturing and mining industries, and approximately three-quarters of the Canadian petroleum industry, were foreign-owned, principally by U.S. investors.

In response to growing concerns in Canada about increasing levels of foreign ownership, the government of Canada introduced the *Foreign Investment Review Act* ("FIRA") in 1973. Under *FIRA*, establishment of new businesses in Canada, direct acquisitions of Canadian businesses by foreign firms and indirect acquisitions of Canadian businesses (involving transfers of ownership of foreign-based parent corporations) were subject to review to determine whether such investments were of "significant benefit" to Canada. During the review process, foreign firms were often encouraged to give undertakings about export performance, import substitution, employment, local sourcing of products, research and development efforts and capital investment plans.

Although *FIRA* was always controversial, U.S. complaints reached a boiling point in the early 1980s when the Canadian government initiated the National Energy Program and proposed more aggressive regulation of foreign investment under *FIRA*. The U.S. government protested and subsequently brought a complaint under the GATT regarding certain of the commitments commonly included in undertakings given to the Canadian government pursuant to *FIRA*. A GATT panel found that Canada had contravened the GATT by urging private firms to commit themselves to source supplies in Canada but ruled that the GATT did not apply to export performance requirements. Canada accepted the GATT ruling, and altered its practices under *FIRA*.

In 1984, the new Conservative government introduced the *Investment Canada Act*, which altered *FIRA* considerably. The *Investment Canada Act* eliminated the requirement of review for the establishment of new businesses except for cultural businesses, and established thresholds of $5 million (Cdn.) and $50 (Cdn.) million for review of direct and indirect acquisitions, respectively. Although the Act's objective is to promote direct investment in Canada, the Investment Canada agency continues to seek undertakings from foreign investors in a limited number of sectors, such as the oil and gas industry.

FOREIGN INVESTMENT UNDER THE FTA

The FTA will reinforce the recent trend toward liberalization of Canadian foreign investment policies and provide greater transparency in the investment restrictions that remain on both sides of the border. Except for the cultural, financial services and transportation industries, future bilateral disputes over investment policies and programs will be subject to the general dispute settlement procedures provided in the FTA.

The investment chapter of the FTA parallels many of the obligations and commitments contained in the services chapter. With the exception of certain changes of the *Investment Canada Act* agreed to in the FTA, all other existing investment restrictions and review requirements are grandfathered and may be amended. Any entirely new investment policies or regulations must be consistent with the principle of national treatment. In other words, any new policies or programs designed to regulate foreign investment in future must not discriminate against U.S. investors. This applies to provincial governments as well as to the federal government. The investment provisions apply to all goods-producing activities and services activities covered in the services chapter, with certain specific exclusions. The transportation industry, the cultural industries, and financial services, except for insurance services, are excluded from the provisions of the investment chapter.

The national treatment obligation concerning future investment policies applies to the establishment of a new business or the acquisition of control of an existing business by a U.S. investor, subject to the provisions of the FTA. Canada has agreed to make certain changes to the *Investment Canada Act* as it applies to investments by U.S. investors. Specifically, Canada has agreed to phase out the screening of indirect acquisitions within three years after the FTA comes into effect, and to raise the threshold for screening of direct acquisitions to $150 million (Cdn.) by 1992 from $5 million (Cdn.) at present. Currently under the *Investment Canada Act*, an acquisition by a non-Canadian is not reviewable if the gross assets of the Canadian business to be acquired are less than $5 million (Cdn.) in the case of a direct acquisition, or less than $50 million (Cdn.) in the case of an indirect acquisition.

In response to U.S. grievances concerning *FIRA's* former propensity to request undertakings, the FTA explicitly precludes the imposition of trade-related performance requirements on U.S. investors. Thus, Investment Canada or any other investment review agency in future may not require U.S. investors to provide undertakings with respect to export performance, import substitution, local sourcing or levels of domestic content. However, an investment review agency, as a condition of approving an investment in future, may require a U.S. investor to give undertakings relating to factors such as research and development efforts or job creation. Minimum domestic equity requirements, except for designated industries, are prohibited in future.

CULTURAL INDUSTRIES

The FTA will not affect the right of the Canadian government, under the *Investment Canada Act*, to review investments by U.S. investors in designated culturally-sensitive Canadian businesses, whether through the establishment of a new business or the acquisition of an existing Canadian business of whatever size. Canadian "cultural industries" are defined as those involved in the production, distribution or sale of books, newspapers, periodicals or music; the production, distribution, sale or exhibition of films, video recordings, audio recordings, or records; and radio and television broadcasting (including cable TV, satellite programming and broadcast networks). As a matter of policy, the Canadian government currently requires new foreign investment in Canadian book publishing and distribution enterprises to be in the form of joint ventures with Canadian control, or in the case of an acquisition of control, to be accompanied by an undertaking to divest control to Canadians within two years at fair market value. Under the terms of the FTA, where the Canadian government requires the forced divestiture of a cultural business, acquired indirectly by a U.S. investor, the government will be obliged to make an offer to purchase the business at fair market value in the absence of Canadian purchasers ready and willing to acquire the business at a reasonable price.

URANIUM, OIL AND GAS INDUSTRIES

The new thresholds for review of acquisitions by U.S. investors under the *Investment Canada Act* will not apply to investments in the uranium and oil and gas industries. Review of investments in those areas will remain subject to existing *Investment Canada Act* thresholds and established policies, which are to be clarified by an exchange of letters between the two governments. The Canadian policy with respect to the uranium industry has been to limit foreign ownership to 33 per cent, but that level was increased effective December 1987 to 49 per cent. The policy in the oil and gas industry is to require undertakings on the part of a foreign firm acquiring a Canadian firm to secure significant Canadian equity participation in the Canadian firm or in selected Canadian resource properties, and to spend substantial sums on exploration and development in Canada. Recently, the Canadian government has indicated that it would not approve the sale of control of an oil and gas company that was in a healthy financial state to non-Canadian investors.

"RIGHT TO EXIT"

As well as providing a right of establishment in future to U.S. investors, the FTA also provides U.S. investors with a "right to exit." Under the FTA, a U.S. investor who owns a Canadian business and wishes to dispose of that business, will be able to sell to a foreign investor outside of the U.S. or Canada more readily than could a Canadian owner. Where a U.S. investor sells a Canadian business to an investor from a third country, the new *Investment Canada Act* thresholds that apply to U.S. investors will apply to that third country investor. The peculiarity of this provision is that a U.S. investor attempting to dispose of a Canadian business may be treated more favourably than a Canadian investor in the same position. A U.S. investor may be able to sell a Canadian business without a requirement of *Investment Canada Act* review to a foreigner from a third country, while a Canadian selling a business of comparable size may not. There may be strong pressures to reduce review requirements for sales of businesses by Canadians to investors from third countries as a result of the U.S. "right to exit" provided for in the FTA.

The FTA also provides for procedures governing expropriation, ensuring due process and fair compensation, as well as ensuring repatriation of earnings subject to laws of general application, such as those relating to insolvency or the imposition of withholding taxes. Where either Canada or the United States decides to expropriate a business owned by an investor of the other country, such expropriation must be for a public purpose, be made on a non-discriminatory basis, be made in accordance with due process of law and be accompanied by prompt payment of adequate and effective compensation at fair market value.

OTHER EXEMPTIONS

It should be noted that the FTA provides certain exclusions from the national treatment obligation with respect to foreign investment. Government procurement practices are explicitly excluded from the investment chapter. As noted above, financial services (with the exception of insurance), transportation services and cultural industries are also excluded from the investment Chapter. Government taxation measures and subsidy programs are also not subject to the national treatment or other investment provisions provided that they do not constitute a means of arbitrary or unjustifiable discrimination against investors from the other country or a disguised restriction on trade.

PRIVATIZATION

If a government decides to privatize a government-owned enterprise in future, it will be permitted to impose national ownership restrictions in determining who may purchase that entity. This applies to enterprises owned, directly or indirectly, by the federal government, a provincial government or a Crown corporation. It also applies to the subsequent privatization of any business enterprise acquired or established by a government in future.

MONOPOLIES

The FTA contains special provisions concerning the maintenance or designation by a federal government of monopolies. It provides that either country may maintain existing, or designate new, monopolies in any relevant market. Prior to designating a new monopoly that might affect the interests of firms in the other country, a government must notify the other country and consult, if requested. Also, where there may be an adverse impact on firms in the other country, the government establishing the monopoly is required to endeavour to regulate the monopoly's operations in such a manner as to minimize the possible adverse impact.

If either country designates a monopoly, it will be obliged to ensure in its regulation or supervision of that monopoly that it does not discriminate in sales against persons or goods of the other country in its monopoly market or use its monopoly position, in another market, to engage in anticompetitive practices that adversely affect a firm of the other country through the discriminatory provision of a good or covered service, cross-subsidization, or predatory behaviour.

The monopolies provisions of the FTA expand on Article XVII of the GATT which deals with state trading enterprises. The GATT and FTA provisions are designed to prevent the use of state-mandated monopolies to circumvent the trade-enhancing measures of those agreements through discriminatory sourcing, pricing and/or distribution practices.

10

Cultural Industries

Cultural industries are, generally speaking, exempt from the FTA provisions on trade in services, investment and temporary entry of business persons. However, bilateral tariffs on products produced or used by a "cultural industry" will be removed as part of the general FTA tariff elimination process. The exemption means that Canadian federal or provincial governments will be able to design new programs or policies in future for these industries that discriminate against U.S. investors or U.S. firms. Where one country establishes a new policy or takes an action that would be inconsistent with the FTA but for the cultural industry exemption, the other country has the right to take measures of "equivalent commercial effect."

"Cultural industries" are broadly defined within the FTA to include the publication, distribution, or sale of books, magazines, periodicals, newspapers, and music; the production, distribution, sale, or exhibition of film, video recordings, audio or music recordings; and radio and TV broadcasting (including cable TV, satellite programming, and broadcast networks).

Under the investment chapter, Canada may continue to impose restrictions on and require review of any U.S. investment in a Canadian cultural business. However, in the event that Canada requires a U.S. firm to divest itself of an interest in a Canadian cultural business, the Canadian government must offer to purchase the business at fair open market value unless a Canadian purchaser is willing to pay full market price.

The government of Canada has agreed to extend the allowable income tax deductions for advertising expenses incurred in placing advertisements in Canadian newspapers or periodicals to those printed or typeset outside of Canada.

In response to another long-standing bilateral irritant, the government of Canada has agreed to extend copyright protection to foreign broadcasts retransmitted in Canada by means of satellite or cable TV services. The Canadian government had announced, in its response to the House Committee Report on Copyright Revision tabled in February 1987, that it intended to include a retransmission right in its revisions to the *Copyright Act*. To date, the Canadian government has introduced Stage One (Bill C-60) of a planned two or three stage revision of the *Copyright Act*. Stage Two, which was to include a retransmission right, has been delayed.

Under the FTA, each country has agreed to provide in its copyright laws that a copyright holder of the other country has a right to be remunerated for any retransmission to the public of a broadcast program where the original transmission to the public is carried in distant signals intended for free, over-the-air reception by the general public. Canada has agreed to amend its *Copyright Act* and have in place a remuneration system by January 1, 1990, at the latest.

Each country is also required to provide in its copyright laws that the authorization of the copyright holder must be obtained for the retransmission of programs to the public, which were not intended in the original transmission for free, over-the-air reception or where, in the case of programs originally intended for free reception by the public, the retransmission has altered the original broadcast or is not simultaneous with it.

The following regulatory measures, in effect in Canada on October 4, 1987, may be maintained:

- requirements that cable companies substitute a higher priority or non-distant TV signal for a simultaneous lower priority or distant, substantially identical, signal;
- prohibitions against retransmission of a distant signal blacked out in the local market or a network signal distributed by a local affiliate;
- prohibitions of programs or advertisements on moral grounds;

- election-related prohibitions;
- pre-emption for urgent and important non-commercial communications;
- cable system licence obligations to substitute non-commercial for commercial material; and
- non-simultaneous transmission in remote locations where simultaneous reception and retransmission are impractical.

As well, the FTA does not preclude the creation of any new regulatory measures to enable a local licensee of copyrighted programs to fully exploit the commercial value of its licence. Canada and the United States have also agreed to establish a joint advisory committee comprised of government and private sector experts to review outstanding issues related to retransmission rights and to make recommendations within 12 months after the FTA comes into effect.

The provisions of the FTA make it clear that broadcasting, publishing, and the production, distribution and sale of artistic and entertainment goods and services are insulated from most of its terms and obligations. The governments of Canada and the provinces may continue to apply, modify, or create new programs to regulate, subsidize or encourage the development of distinctive Canadian cultural products and services and to restrict entry or investment by U.S. entertainment enterprises.

The commitment to provide a retransmission right in Canadian copyright law largely reflects existing Canadian government policy. The FTA also contains general exemptions to permit the continuation of existing Canadian Radio-Television and Telecommunications Commission ("CRTC") cable regulations and the imposition of new broadcasting regulations affecting networks, cable TV, and satellite broadcasts, where necessary, to protect Canadian broadcast and cable licensees.

The most important provision relating to cultural industries is the ability of the United States to respond to new Canadian cultural protection measures that are inconsistent with the FTA with measures of "equivalent commercial effect." Currently, the United States can take retaliatory action against discriminatory foreign government practices that restrict or that burden U.S. exports of goods or services under section 301 of the *Trade Act of 1974*. In 1984, the United States took such retaliatory action against section 19 of the Canadian *Income Tax Act* (or Bill C-58), which disallows deductions for advertising expenses incurred by Canadians in U.S. newspapers or periodicals, radio or TV directed at the Canadian market, by enacting mirror legislation. Such disputes in future would be dealt with bilaterally under the dispute settlement provisions of the FTA.

11

Trade in Services

BREAKING NEW GROUND

Trade in services has become an increasingly significant feature of the world economy. In 1985, world trade in services was estimated to be in the range of $400-$500 billion annually, about one-quarter of the amount of world trade in goods. In Canada and the United States, services account for an overwhelming percentage of gross domestic product and a major source of employment growth. In 1984, Canada-U.S. trade in services represented approximately $20 billion.

Despite its significance in the world economy, international services trade, by and large, is not regulated by international agreements. The GATT is focused primarily on trade in goods. As a result of U.S. initiatives, some of the 1979 Tokyo Round agreements include provisions covering some goods-related services trade. The United States has emphasized trade in services as a priority in the Uruguay Round of multilateral trade negotiations currently under way. The FTA represents an important first step in the adoption of general principles governing trade in services worldwide. The FTA, although groundbreaking, is also cautious in its approach to the regulation of bilateral services trade. It is cautious because it applies only to "covered services" and does not, for the most part, require changes to existing measures.

COVERED SERVICES

Covered services under the FTA include agriculture and forestry, mining, construction, distributive trades, insurance and real estate, and commercial services. The latter includes cleaning services; advertising and promotional services; collection agency services; telephone answering services; services to buildings; equipment rental and leasing services; personnel supply services; hotel services; professional services; commercial, economic, marketing, and statistical services; public relations services; repair and maintenance services; business consulting services; management services; computer services; telecommunications services; and tourism services.

In the area of professional services, the FTA covers engineering; architectural and surveying services; accounting and auditing services; scientific and technical services; librarian services; and agricultural consulting services.

EXEMPTIONS

Financial services are dealt with in a separate chapter of the FTA. The general services chapter does not affect financial services, with the exception of insurance. Transportation services and cultural industries are also excluded from the services chapter, as are basic telecommunications services (such as telephone services), doctors, dentists, lawyers, childcare and government services (such as health, education and social services).

NATIONAL TREATMENT

The obligations contained in the FTA are not as extensive as some of the U.S. proposals for regulation of international services trade being advanced in the Uruguay Round of multilateral trade negotiations. Only in the areas of financial services, tourism, architecture, and enhanced telecommunications services (dealt with in specific chapters or sectoral annexes) will the FTA require any changes to existing laws, regulations or policies.

With respect to the future, the FTA establishes the GATT principle of national treatment as the primary obligation in the services area. Subject to certain qualifications, Canada and the United States have agreed to treat persons or firms of the other country no less favourably than their own nationals with respect to the provision of covered services. Under the FTA, provision of covered services includes:

- production, distribution, sale, marketing and delivery of a covered service and the purchase or use thereof;
- access to, and use of, domestic distribution systems;
- the establishment of a commercial presence (other than an investment) for the purpose of distributing, marketing, delivering or facilitating the covered service; and
- any investment for the provision of a covered service and any activity associated with the provision of a covered service.

The obligation to provide national treatment applies to provincial and state governments as well as to the federal governments of both countries. Governments, however, will not be restricted from treating nationals of the other country differently from their own nationals where the difference in treatment is no greater than is justified for prudential, fiduciary, health and safety or consumer protection reasons. Where a government proposes a new policy that discriminates against nationals of the other country, it must notify the other country prior to implementing the new policy, and must be able to justify it as being no greater than necessary for one of the above public policy objectives.

SUBSIDIES AND GOVERNMENT PROCUREMENT

Beyond the basic national treatment obligation, there is a requirement that neither country may introduce any measure that constitutes a means of arbitrary or unjustifiable discrimination against persons of the other country or a disguised restriction on bilateral trade in covered services. The FTA provides explicitly that the services chapter imposes no obligations or rights concerning government procurement practices or the use of subsidies. In other words, in a covered services area such as advertising, a government that chose to specify that government contracts for advertising services would be granted only to locally-based companies would not be affected by the terms of the FTA. Also, if a government decided to provide a new subsidy program or tax benefit to encourage the provision of accounting services in a particular region, it would not have to allow nationals of the other country equal opportunity to qualify for benefits under that program. The services obligations also do not apply to any new taxation measure as long as it does not constitute a means of arbitrary or unjustifiable discrimination or a disguised restriction on trade between the two countries.

The benefits of freer trade in services are exclusively reserved for persons that are nationals or controlled by nationals of either Canada or the United States. Both countries have reserved the right to deny the benefits of the services chapter to firms that are owned or controlled, directly or indirectly, by persons from a third country.

LICENSING AND CERTIFICATION

A special obligation has been included in the FTA governing licensing and certification procedures. Both countries have agreed in principle that licensing and certification requirements for professional or other services should relate to matters of competency or the ability to provide a service and should not have the effect of impairing the access of nationals of either country to provide their services in the other country. To that end, Canada and the United States have agreed to work together to develop methods for mutual recognition of licensing and certification requirements for the provision of covered services by persons of either country.

IMPACT OF THE SERVICES CHAPTER

Understanding the national treatment obligation is critical to under-standing the services chapter of the FTA. The obligation to extend national treatment to nationals of the other country means that Canada and the United States have agreed to treat providers of services from the other country no less favourably than domestic providers of the same services in like circumstances. However, if there are important health, safety, prudential, fiduciary or consumer protection reasons for treating firms of the other country differently, governments may do so as long as the treatment is equivalent in effect. Existing laws and regulations that are discriminatory may be maintained but, if amended, there is an obligation not to make them more restrictive.

The national treatment obligation will not in itself lead to the harmonization of regulation of services on both sides of the border. In fact, in the annex on enhanced telecommunications services, it is explicitly recognized that the two countries will have different regulatory systems with different procedures for setting rates, licensing providers of services and otherwise regulating the provision of services. The primary obligation for regulators in future will be to ensure that Canadian and U.S. nationals providing covered services in the same country are treated equivalently.

Canada and the United States both recognize that the FTA rules on services trade, although a significant first step, are not an end in themselves. The two countries have agreed to cooperate further to develop new rules and to extend the obligations of the services chapter by negotiating further sectoral annexes and modifying or eliminating existing measures that are contrary to the FTA principles.

FINANCIAL SERVICES

Federally-regulated financial services are covered in a separate chapter of the FTA. The services chapter applies only to insurance services, and not to other financial services. Provincial or state regulation of securities dealers, loan and trust companies, near banks and other financial institutions is not covered by the FTA.

Canada has already started the process of deregulation in the financial services sector. As a result, the strict separation that traditionally existed between the functions of banks, insurance companies, trust and loan companies and securities dealers is being largely relaxed. Although some U.S. states are beginning to permit some cross-ownership of financial institutions, there has been no major regulatory overhaul of U.S. federal banking legislation as yet.

The FTA has accommodated this regulatory disparity by imposing rather different obligations on the United States and Canada in the area of financial services. With respect to future regulatory changes to the *Glass-Steagall Act* and other federal legislation, the United States has agreed to accord Canadian-controlled financial institutions the same treatment as their U.S.-controlled counterparts. Canada has agreed to provide U.S.-controlled financial institutions with the opportunity to expand through the acquisition of other financial service businesses as a result of the Canadian deregulation process. The former commitment involves future consideration; the latter commitment involves modifications to existing laws and policies.

Despite the strict separation of powers among the different types of financial institutions in the United States, banks are currently authorized to underwrite and deal in debt obligations of, or guaranteed by, the United States of America or its political subdivisions. The FTA would permit domestic and foreign banks to trade in a similar way in the debt instruments of Canadian federal and provincial governments. Future U.S. issues of provincial hydro-electric utility bonds, for example, could be floated through U.S. banks rather than exclusively through underwriting houses.

Foreign banks operating in the United States have enjoyed favoured treatment in that they have been allowed to expand beyond the limits of a state in circumstances where their U.S.-owned competitors are often confined to a single jurisdiction. This privilege is currently scheduled to be reviewed in 1988. The FTA provides Canadian-controlled banks with a standstill guarantee that they will not, in any event, lose their existing rights under the *International Banking Act of 1978* to operate in more than one jurisdiction.

For its part, Canada will be required by the FTA to amend a series of federal statutes that impose foreign ownership restrictions that inhibit the sale of a substantial interest in a bank, a life insurance company, a sales finance company, a loan company or a trust company to non-Canadians. Generally speaking, these statutes prohibit the entry in the books of the financial institution of any transfer of shares that would result in 10 per cent or more of the shares being held by an individual who is not ordinarily resident in Canada, or by a legal entity controlled by any such individuals. The entry of a transfer of shares of such an institution is also generally prohibited if the result would be that a number of non-Canadians would hold, in the aggregate, 25 per cent or more of the outstanding shares. Existing Canadian federal legislation will have to be amended to make these prohibitions inapplicable to U.S. or U.S.-controlled investors.

The Canadian government has recently proposed new legislation that would require approval for any transfer of shares in an insurance company, a loan company or a trust company that would result in any one person, together with associates, holding 10 per cent or more of the outstanding shares of any class of shares of the financial institution. This requirement is not specifically related to foreign-ownership concerns. Rather, it relates to concerns about corporate concentration. The FTA would prohibit the use of this review power in a discriminatory manner so as to prevent U.S.-controlled entities from acquiring shares in a Canadian financial institution, while allowing Canadian-controlled entities to make such an investment.

There is a large gap in the FTA rules with respect to U.S. investment in Canadian financial institutions as they will not apply to any measure of a provincial government. Provincial governments play a very significant role in Canada in the incorporation and regulation of financial institutions other than banks. Many such institutions are incorporated provincially. Some provinces impose their own foreign ownership restrictions upon entities constituted under provincial law; for example, Ontario loan and trust companies are subject to the same ten per cent (and 25 per cent in the aggregate) restriction on transfers of shares to foreigners, as currently applies to federally-incorporated loan and trust companies. That provincial limitation will not have to be changed as a consequence of the FTA.

The provinces also exercise regulatory jurisdiction over non-bank financial institutions that carry on business within their territories irrespective of the jurisdiction of incorporation of such an institution. Even a federally-incorporated and licensed insurance, loan or trust company must hold a provincial licence in most Canadian provinces in which it carries on business; it cannot operate as of right under the authority of its federal licence. Although the provinces do not require any degree of Canadian ownership as a condition for initial or continued licensing now, the FTA would not preclude them from creating such a condition in future, except in relation to insurance services. The services chapter of the FTA would prohibit new provincial measures relating to the provision of insurance services that discriminate against entities owned or controlled by U.S. nationals.

Finally, the financial services chapter of the FTA will eliminate some of the restrictions under the Canadian *Bank Act* on the operation and expansion of foreign bank subsidiaries (Schedule B banks) as they apply to U.S.-owned entities. In particular, in the case of Schedule B banks that are subsidiaries of U.S. banks:

- the amount of capital is not to be constrained by the umbrella limit on the domestic assets of foreign bank subsidiaries;
- the opening of branches is not to require ministerial approval; and
- the transfer of loans from a bank subsidiary to its parent is to be permitted subject to prudential requirements of general application.

In summary, the financial services chapter represents an incomplete, piecemeal approach to some issues in the financial services area that are not the same on both sides of the border. The two countries explicitly recognize that this chapter does not signify their "mutual satisfaction . . . concerning the treatment of their respective financial institutions" and that laws and policies should evolve to the mutual benefit of both countries as the rules governing financial markets are liberalized. Further bilateral negotiations relating to financial services will be the responsibility of officials of the Canadian Department of Finance and the U.S. Department of Treasury. The general dispute settlement mechanisms of the FTA will not apply to the financial services sector.

TELECOMMUNICATIONS AND COMPUTER SERVICES

A sectoral annex to the general services chapter of the FTA provides specific commitments with respect to "enhanced" telecommunications and computer services. For regulatory purposes, "enhanced" telecommunications services have been distinguished from "basic" services. The Canadian Radio-Television and Telecommunications Commission (the "CRTC") and the U.S. Federal Communications Commission (the "FCC") have adopted essentially similar definitions of "basic" services as the provision of direct transmission capacity. Both regulatory agencies include the following in their definitions of basic service: speed, code, and protocol conversion that occurs within the carrier's network as long as the transmission parameters do not alter the nature of the transmission. "Enhanced services" are defined, by the CRTC and the FCC, as everything else, and include the storage, manipulation, and transmission of data on a commercial basis. The FTA incorporates the same definitions of basic and enhanced services as those employed by the CRTC and the FCC.

Computer services are defined with some precision in this annex as services, whether or not conveyed over the basic telecommunications network, which involve generating, acquiring, storing, transforming, processing, retrieving, utilizing or making available information in a computerized form. A number of such services are listed, including computer programming, prepackaged software, computer-integrated systems design, computer processing and data preparation. This list makes it clear that the annex, while primarily directed at ensuring a free, non-discriminatory flow in computing services that ride the telecommunications networks of each country, also comprehends the direct provision of computer services.

Insofar as the direct provision of computing services is concerned, this annex is an important complement to the general rules on commercial presence in the services chapter and the chapter on temporary entry for business persons, which will ease transborder movement of computer services as well as sales management, installation and maintenance personnel.

The provisions of the services chapter will apply to the following regulatory measures relating to enhanced telecommunications and computer services:

- access to, and use of, basic telecommunications services including local and message toll or long distance service, private-line or leased line services, dedicated voice and data networks;

- resale and shared use of basic telecommunications services;
- the purchase and lease, or attachment, of customer premises equipment (e.g., telephone sets, private branch exchanges, data terminals);
- regulatory definitions of basic and enhanced services;
- technical standards for certification, testing or approval procedures (subject to the product standards chapter); and
- the movement of information across borders and access to data bases or related information stored in the other country.

This annex provides that Canada and the United States will maintain existing access for nationals of the other country to basic services for the provision of enhanced and computer services, and maintain or introduce effective measures to prevent anti-competitive conduct by a monopoly telecommunication carrier in the enhanced services market, either directly or through dealings with its affiliates that adversely affect a firm in the other country. Anti-competitive conduct is defined as including cross-subsidization, predatory conduct, and the discriminatory provision of access to basic telecommunications facilities or services.

This annex confirms existing regulatory policies on enhanced telecommunications services in both Canada and the United States and does not require any specific changes to existing policies or practices. It does not require the introduction of any more telecommunications service competition than already exists in federally-regulated telecommunications markets in Canada and the United States. The annex may, however, create an incentive to bring Canadian and U.S. regulatory measures aimed at preventing anti-competitive behaviour by monopoly telecommunications carriers more into line.

Provincial telecommunications regulators have, on the other hand, lagged behind the CRTC in allowing enhanced services competition. The FTA may create pressures on them to catch up to the CRTC, thereby establishing a national enhanced telecommunications services market in Canada. Generally, U.S. state regulators have adopted a competitive stance to enhanced services similar to the FCC's policy.

An important provision of this annex is that Canada and the United States have agreed not to impose new limits on transborder data flows for industrial development purposes. Current restrictions on data processing contained in the Canadian *Bank Act*, however, will be maintained. The possibility of adapting measures to prevent the storage and processing of Canadian-originating information in the United

States in order to stimulate a domestic data processing industry has been a recurrent theme in Canadian government circles over the last 20 years.

The provisions of this annex are intended to work together with the accelerated reductions in tariffs on computing equipment. The greater certainty of non-discriminatory network access for enhanced services in both countries may encourage greater marketing efforts by computing equipment firms in each country.

ARCHITECTURE

A separate annex to the services chapter will apply to measures relating to the mutual recognition of professional standards and criteria for the licensing and conduct of architects and the provision of architectural services.

Canada and the United States have agreed to endorse and promote the adoption of mutually acceptable professional standards and criteria relating to professional training, licensing, conduct and ethics for architects. The Royal Architectural Institute of Canada and the American Institute of Architects have undertaken to develop, in consultation with the appropriate regulatory bodies, mutually acceptable professional standards and criteria prior to the end of 1989.

Upon receiving the recommendations of these professional associations, Canada and the United States have agreed to encourage provincial and state regulatory authorities to accept and adopt their recommendations on mutual recognition of architects.

TOURISM

Tourism services are covered in another sectoral annex to the services chapter. The services covered by this annex include travel agencies, travel insurance, international passenger transportation, hotel reservation services, transportation terminal services, tour operations, and related retail and rental services.

In this annex, Canada and the United States have agreed to maintain, in future, the free and open access both countries provide now to tourists from the other country. The real purpose of this annex is not to eliminate any bilateral restrictions on tourism trade, but to set an example for other countries in the Uruguay Round of multilateral trade negotiations.

In particular, Canada and the United States have agreed that neither country will impose restrictions in its territory on the promotion of tourism opportunities by the other country or by its provincial, state or local governments. Any departure or arrival fees charged by either country to tourists from the other must be applied equally to nationals of the country imposing the fees and be limited to the approximate cost of services rendered. Any restrictions imposed by one country on the value of tourism services that its residents or visitors to its territory may purchase from persons of the other country must conform to provisions of the Agreement of the International Monetary Fund ("IMF"), which prohibit the imposition of restrictions on international currency payments and transfers without the approval of the IMF, and which prohibit currency practices that discriminate against other parties to the IMF Agreement.

Adoption of the principles contained in this annex will not represent any change in the *status quo*. Currently, neither country imposes departure or arrival fees or currency restrictions on tourists from the other country. There is now a virtually unrestricted market in tourism between Canada and the United States. The two countries have also agreed to consult at least once a year to identify and eliminate impediments to tourist trade and to find ways to facilitate increased tourism between them.

12

Temporary Entry Of Business Persons

THE EXISTING LAW

A general easing of restrictions on the cross-border movement of business personnel between Canada and the United States will be an important factor in facilitating the free flow of goods and services between the two countries. In the last few years, restrictions on the entry of consultants and professionals as well as sales representatives and maintenance personnel have been a significant non-tariff barrier to trade. The FTA establishes a special regime for temporary entry of Canadian and U.S. citizens into each other's territory for business purposes. No changes are contemplated in the immigration rules that determine who will be granted permanent resident status by either country.

On the Canadian side, there are a number of regulations and policies that will have to be changed as they apply to U.S. business persons engaging in temporary business activities in Canada. Under the Canadian *Immigration Regulations*, an individual who is neither a citizen nor a permanent resident (landed immigrant) of Canada may not work in Canada without first obtaining an employment authorization, commonly called a "work permit." There are a few exceptions to this requirement, but none that favour a person who is employed or self-employed outside Canada or who will not be paid from Canadian sources for his or her services performed in Canada.

Under existing law, a U.S. employee of a U.S. business enterprise, a U.S. entrepreneur or a U.S. professional would normally have to obtain a work permit to carry out any business function in Canada. The harshness of this is only alleviated by Canadian immigration officials stretching the exceptions or turning a blind eye. The difficulty that a visitor faces in satisfying the work permit requirement is not just the cost ($50) and the paper burden but, more importantly, meeting the usual condition of having to persuade an officer of Employment Canada to certify that job opportunities for Canadian citizens or permanent residents will not be adversely affected by the issue of the permit.

BUSINESS VISITOR RULES

The FTA would require Canada to grant temporary entry, without the necessity of a work permit, to any citizen of the United States who is engaged in trade in goods or services or in investment activities and who comes to Canada in the course of performing certain occupational functions and for certain business purposes, all as specifically prescribed by the FTA. The listed occupations involve some degree of skill and, in most cases, the type of activity carried out in Canada must be limited either in its nature or in that the principal beneficiary must be U.S.-based. In particular, these occupations include:

- technical or market researchers carrying out research for an enterprise located in the United States;
- purchasing, production management, financial services and supervisory personnel involved in transactions for an enterprise located in the United States;
- sales representatives taking orders for goods or services;
- buyers purchasing for an enterprise located in the United States;
- installers and maintenance personnel performing certain after-sales services in respect of equipment purchased from an enterprise located outside Canada; and
- public relations and advertising personnel consulting with business associates.

Some of these categories already have the benefit, in part at least, of existing exceptions to the work permit requirement under the

Immigration Regulations; others are brand new exceptions and will clearly reflect special treatment for U.S. business visitors to Canada.

As there are also FTA provisions relating to intra-company transferees, referred to below, we assume that the business visitor rules will not apply to U.S. citizens who have been seconded for a period of time to a Canadian affiliate or a branch of their U.S.-based employer. Such an individual would probably be treated as having ceased to work for an enterprise located in the United States, for the purposes of the business visitor categories, and therefore as eligible to enter Canada, without an immigration visa, only if qualified under the intra-company transferee rules. In fact, the FTA does not make it clear what length of stay or what number of periodic visits may be enjoyed by a business visitor or, indeed, when the privilege of temporary entry may be taken to have been abused in that a temporary stay has become, in fact, a long-term settlement.

U.S. business visitors to Canada may be subject to exclusion, as are other visitors, on security or health grounds. But otherwise, all that may be required is proof of U.S. citizenship and demonstration of the purpose of the visit in terms that fall within one of the designated occupational categories.

In certain other situations not coming within the business visitor rules, Canada will be obliged to issue work permits to U.S. citizens engaged in trading in goods or services or in investment activities, enabling them to enter and work in Canada under the authority of such a permit. A work permit may be issued at a port of entry (a border crossing, an airport or a port) to a U.S. citizen and need not be secured in advance from a Canadian immigration post outside the country.

When a work permit is required to be issued to a U.S. citizen by the terms of the FTA there will be no underlying requirement that an officer of Employment Canada first certify that in his or her opinion there will be no adverse effect on employment opportunities for Canadian citizens or permanent residents. The groups that will get the benefit of certification — free (validation exempt) entry are intra-company transferees, traders and investors and professionals.

INTRA-COMPANY TRANSFEREES

Intra-company transferees are U.S. citizens seeking temporary entry into Canada to work, within their corporate or business group, in a capacity that is managerial, executive or involves specialized knowledge. They must be destined to work or render services in Canada for an employer for whom they have worked continuously for at least one year immediately prior to entry, or an affiliate or subsidiary of such an employer.

Canadian immigration policies currently permit the entry of senior executive or managerial staff on an intra-company transfer basis without any employment certification. However, the FTA would appear to contemplate the broadening of this policy insofar as it affects U.S. transferees, so as to cover managerial and executive personnel who are not top management, and personnel utilizing "specialized knowledge" who are not managers of any kind. The latter description may prove to be particularly elastic — capable of describing a broad spectrum of experienced and skilled workers. Under the present Canadian policy transferees must be assigned to work at permanent and continuing establishments of their employer in Canada. As a result, employees intending to work on construction or other engineering sites or projects are not eligible currently for consideration as intra-company transferees. The FTA would preclude any such blanket exclusion for U.S. citizens in the future.

TRADERS AND INVESTORS

The trader and investor classification under the FTA covers, first, U.S. citizens carrying on a substantial trade in goods or services who are seeking temporary entry to Canada in a capacity that is supervisory or executive or involves essential skills. The trade in question must be primarily between Canada and the United States. Since sales representatives, purchasers of goods and services, and certain services personnel may enter with even fewer impediments as business visitors, the number of U.S. citizens seeking temporary entry to Canada as traders may not be significant.

This classification, in its second element, covers U.S. citizens who would enter Canada on a temporary basis solely to develop and direct the operations of an enterprise in which they have invested, or are in the process of investing, a substantial amount of capital. The investment need not involve control of a Canadian enterprise and, indeed, could be a debt rather than an equity investment. It is probably sufficient if the capital invested is a substantial sum in the abstract, although some might argue that it must be substantial in relation to the overall capitalization of the enterprise.

PROFESSIONALS

Finally, U.S. citizens who are engaged in professions of a kind described in the FTA may enter Canada on a temporary basis. As is evident from other chapters of the FTA, this does not mean that they would then be entitled, as of right and without holding any relevant federal or provincial certification, to carry out professional activities of such a nature and duration as to constitute professional practice in a Canadian jurisdiction.

The professions included for the purposes of this classification are not just those occupational categories that have been traditionally recognized as professions or that involve a substantial measure of self-governance, but extend to such occupations as that of hotel manager and technical publication writer. In some instances, a certain minimum academic or work experience is essential and, in a few cases, the type of professional activity that may be carried out is limited, for example, U.S. physicians may only be engaged in teaching or research in Canada.

Professionals may be asked, at the port of entry into Canada, for proof of citizenship and documentation demonstrating that they are engaged in one of the listed professions and describing the purpose of entry.

WORK PERMITS

As in the case of U.S business visitors or any other visitors, those U.S. citizens who will be entitled to enter and work in Canada on the basis of a work permit issued on a certification-free basis will be subject to general security and health restrictions.

A work permit is usually issued, in accordance with current Canadian practice, for a period of up to one year, subject to further extensions. After a permit holder has been in Canada for three years or so, there is likely to be some reluctance on the part of an immigration officer to grant a further renewal, particularly without certification by an officer of Employment Canada. As in the case of business visitors, the FTA is silent as to when a temporary sojourn may be properly characterized as having become permanent. Since the FTA contemplates the issue of work permits to intra-company transferees, traders and investors, and professionals, it may be assumed that the present timetable for that instrument of approval will, at least, be acceptable.

An individual who has a complaint about being denied entry contrary to the provisions of the FTA must use the administrative appeal mechanisms available under Canadian or U.S. immigration law. If immigration authorities of one country engage in a pattern of practice contrary to the FTA, the other country may invoke the FTA dispute settlement provisions to resolve the problem.

ENTRY INTO THE UNITED STATES

We have described the FTA provisions permitting temporary entry of U.S. citizens into Canada for business purposes. The obligations upon the United States in relation to Canadian business persons are essentially reciprocal. There are some technical variations because of differences in regulations under the Canadian *Immigration Act* and the U.S. *Immigration and Nationality Act*. It should be noted that preferential admission into either country is open only to citizens of the other country and not to permanent residents or landed immigrants.

The FTA represents a first step toward the freer movement of business personnel between Canada and the United States. The objective of the FTA is to reduce the unnecessary harassment that many business travellers experience at the border. Over the longer term, a consultative mechanism will be established, at the level of immigration officials, to develop measures for further facilitating temporary entry of business persons between Canada and the United States on a reciprocal basis.

13

Trade Remedies

EMERGENCY ACTIONS

In the FTA, Canada and the United States have agreed to substantive changes in the "safeguards" or "escape clause" trade laws applied by either country under Article XIX of the GATT. The *Shakes and Shingles* and *Speciality Steel* cases are recent examples of such U.S. actions. Under these domestic laws, the United States or Canada can impose border measures, including duties or quotas, on imports of a product from foreign countries if imports are increasing in such a manner as to be causing or threatening to cause serious injury to a domestic industry. These are "fair trade" laws; they involve no allegation of unfair trade practices, such as dumping or subsidization. They are intended to provide a domestic industry with temporary relief, an escape hatch, where imports are increasing to such an extent as to create serious adjustment problems for that industry.

In the FTA, Canada and the United States have agreed to a new two-track system for such emergency actions. A special bilateral track has been established to deal with increases in imports caused by a reduction of duties made under the FTA. Where increasing imports of a product from the other country alone are found to constitute a substantial cause of serious injury to a domestic industry, the importing country may suspend the reduction of any duty on that product under the FTA or increase the duty to the lower of the current Most-Favoured-Nation rate or pre-FTA levels. The imposition of emergency relief measures under the bilateral track is limited to a period of three years, may be taken only in the transition period (i.e., until 1998), and may be taken only once for any particular product. The bilateral emergency action provisions are intended to provide temporary relief for domestic industries from severe unforeseen adjustment difficulties.

Substantial changes affecting global emergency actions involving imports from several countries have also been made. Currently, Canadian and U.S. domestic law permits the imposition of measures, such a duties or quotas, against imports of a particular product from several countries where a sudden surge in those imports is causing or is threatening to cause serious injury to a domestic industry.

Canadian industries have been swept up many times in the past in U.S. section 201 cases where Canadian exports of a product under investigation represented less than 5 per cent of all imports into the United States. Such cases have included steel products, agricultural products, motor vehicles, metal castings, footwear, tuna fish, apple juice and television sets.

The FTA provides that in a U.S. section 201 case, for example, involving imports from several countries, imports of that product from Canada are to be excluded unless they are "substantial" and "contribute importantly" to the serious injury or threat thereof caused by imports from all sources. For imports from Canada to be "substantial', in such a case, they must represent more than 5 to 10 per cent of total imports. These new standards should reduce the number of U.S. section 201 cases involving imports from several countries in which Canadian industries have been "side-swiped." Also, where U.S. section 201 measures are imposed on imports from Canada, they must not restrict the flow of Canadian products below the trend of those imports over a reasonable recent base period with an allowance for growth.

The FTA also requires each country to notify and, where requested, consult with the other prior to imposing an emergency action measure on imports from the other country. A major complaint of the government of Canada in the 1986 *Shakes and Shingles* case was that the President did not notify the Prime Minister that he was going to impose a 35 per cent duty on imports from Canada.

Where one country objects to a duty, quota or other emergency action measure imposed by the other country, the formal dispute settlement mechanisms of the FTA may be invoked. The two countries are first to attempt to resolve the matter by government-to-government consultations. Where they are unable to do so, the country affected may apply to the Canada-U.S. Trade Commission for the establishment of a binding arbitration panel to determine the matter. Any decision made by a binational arbitration panel concerning an emergency action measure is final and binding on both countries and their agencies. The ability of an international panel to review and make binding decisions concerning a country's application of emergency action measures under Article XIX of the GATT is unprecedented in the GATT or other international trade agreements.

ANTIDUMPING AND COUNTERVAILING DUTY PROVISIONS

Canada and the United States have agreed in the FTA to develop and implement, within a period of 5 to 7 years, a substitute system of antidumping and countervailing duty laws to be applicable in both countries. This is an important commitment. Many studies, including the Royal Commission on the Economic Union and Development Prospects for Canada (the "Macdonald Commission"), have recommended that U.S. and Canadian trade laws be substantially changed so that they do not continue to cause uncertainty and harassment for Canadian and U.S. exporters. A joint Working Group will be established to develop the new system of laws. If a new system of trade laws is not implemented within the agreed time frame, either country may terminate the FTA on six months' notice.

In the interim, both countries will continue to apply their own domestic antidumping and countervailing duty laws and may change those laws. This means that Canadian and U.S. firms may continue to bring antidumping or countervailing duty cases against imports from the other country under the current domestic laws and procedures.

Each country's right to apply and amend its domestic laws is subject to important new constraints. A new binational panel procedure will be established to take the place of judicial review by the courts of final antidumping and countervailing duty orders in both Canada and the United States. At the request of either country, a binational panel will be selected from a roster of panelists to review a final antidumping or countervailing duty order made by the International Trade Administration of the Department of Commerce or the International Trade Commission in the United States, or the Department of National Revenue-Customs and Excise or the Canadian Import Tribunal in Canada. The panel's task will be to determine if the agency concerned made its decision in accordance with domestic law. The binational panel would be required to apply the standard of judicial review applicable in the country where the investigation took place. The decision of the panel will be binding on the member countries and their agencies.

Only the two federal governments may initiate the new binational panel review procedures. The FTA, recognizing that antidumping and countervailing duty cases are essentially private actions, has expressly assured access by private parties to the binational panel review mechanism. Where a private party involved in an antidumping or countervailing duty investigation requests that its government commence a binational panel review on its behalf, that government is required under the FTA to comply.

The new binational panel review process offers several major advantages for private firms over the current system. First of all, the binational panel process will reduce the time for final resolution of antidumping and countervailng duty cases. Appeals of U.S. cases through the courts can take from two to four years. The FTA binational panel procedure will be subject to a limit of 315 days measured from the end of the agency proceedings. This maximum time limit should reduce the potential for open-ended delays in individual cases and provide private firms with greater certainty and security than is available under the current system. Another practical advantage of the new procedure is the use of five binational panelists rather than a single judge as is the case currently in the U.S. system. The binational composition of the review panels should encourage a full airing of different interpretations of U.S. and Canadian trade laws.

The binational review procedure will also provide a cost advantage for small- and medium-sized businesses in both countries. At present, firms or trade associations that decide to appeal antidumping or countervailing duty decisions to the courts must pay for it themselves. Under the FTA, the binational panel reviews will be initiated and conducted by the federal governments. Therefore, a small- or medium-sized business or trade association that would not otherwise have been able to afford the expense of challenging an agency ruling in the courts would, after the FTA comes into effect, be able to have its case presented by its government. Private firms that choose to make representations and appear before a binational panel on their own behalf will be permitted to do so. The agency involved will also be able to make representations to the binational panel reviewing its decision.

The FTA will also establish a mechanism designed to deter future protectionist changes in either country's trade laws. Neither the United States or Canada will be permitted to amend its antidumping or countervailing duty laws as they affect the other country unless the amending legislation states specifically that it will apply to the other country, there has been prior notification to the other country, and the proposed amendments are consistent with the GATT, the Antidumping Code and the Subsidies and Countervailing Duties Code, and with the object and purpose of the FTA. Where the other country objects to a country's proposed amendments to its trade laws, government-to-government consultations are to be initiated. If consultations fail to achieve a solution, the other country may request that a binational panel be appointed to review and issue a declaratory opinion on the proposed amendments. Where a binational panel issues a declaration recommending changes to the proposed amendments, the two governments are required to enter into compulsory consultations for a period of 90 days during which they are to seek a mutually agreeable solution. If the country proposing the amendments fails to comply with a panel's opinion, and no mutual resolution is reached within nine months, the other country may enact mirror legislation or terminate the FTA upon 60 days' notice.

The dispute settlement mechanisms embodied in the FTA should prove important to the development of a common Canada-U.S. system of trade laws. The binational antidumping and countervailing duty panels, in particular, should help to ensure that legislative developments in both countries remain consistent with the objectives and purposes of the FTA and with the principles of the GATT. The binational dispute settlement mechanisms should also help to provide a period of stability to assist in the development of a common body of trade laws. The binational panels may encourage the creation of a body of experts in each country with experience actually applying the laws of the other country to disputes in specific cases. The development of such a body of expertise could assist in the negotiation of a common system of trade laws.

INSTITUTIONAL PROVISIONS

The FTA also establishes institutional mechanisms designed to promote the avoidance or settlement of trade-related disputes between Canada and the United States. Currently, the two countries do not have a formal bilateral process for notification, consultation, or resolution of disputes affecting trade. Apart from the GATT, there are no formal mechanisms for resolving such disputes. Although the GATT procedures are being improved, there is considerable opinion in the world trading community that the GATT dispute resolution mechanisms suffer from lengthy delays, hesitation on the part of governments to use them, and a GATT focus on negotiated solutions in many cases.

Under the FTA, a Canada–United States Trade Commission (the "Commission") will be established to supervise the proper implementation of the FTA, to resolve any disputes that may arise over its interpretation or application, to oversee its further elaboration, and to consider any other matter that may affect its operation. The Commission will be composed of representatives of both member countries, and will be headed by Cabinet ministers responsible for international trade or their designees. It will have the authority to create subsidiary *ad hoc* committees or working groups to investigate and resolve disputes or to negotiate and develop new rules as provided for in the FTA.

The institutional provisions of the FTA will not apply to disputes arising under the chapter relating to binational review of antidumping or countervailing duty cases or the financial services chapter.

Essential to the proper functioning of the FTA are its provisions for notification and consultation. Each country is required to provide written notice to the other country of any existing or proposed legislation, regulations, governmental procedures or practices that might materially affect the operation of the FTA. It is important to recognize that any governmental measure or action that may affect the object and purpose of the FTA would be required to be notified. At the request of the country affected, the country proposing the measure is required to provide information in response to any questions asked.

In addition, each country may request formal government-to-government consultations with respect to any existing or proposed measure, whether or not it has been notified, that it considers would affect the operation of the FTA. The establishment in the FTA of institutionalized channels for government-to-government communications concerning any government measures that may affect trade is an important new development in Canada-U.S. trade relations.

Where a problem arises, Canada and the United States are directed to make every attempt to arrive at a mutually satisfactory resolution by government-to-government consultations. If they fail to resolve the matter, either country may apply in writing to the Commission. The Commission is required to convene within 10 days to endeavour to resolve the dispute. The Commission may use a range of different mechanisms to reach a mutually satisfactory resolution of the dispute. It may appoint a special committee or a working group or call on technical advisors or on the assistance of a mediator to achieve a consensus solution. Where a dispute has been referred to the Commission and there has been no resolution within 30 days, the Commission is required, upon the request of either country, to establish a panel of experts to consider the matter. All disputes involving "emergency actions" taken under that chapter of the FTA must, and any other dispute the Commission selects may, be referred to a binding arbitration panel.

There are explicit time limits at every stage of the dispute resolution process. In any case involving an "emergency action", or any other case where the Commission has referred the matter to binding arbitration, the decision of the panel will be final. In other cases, the Commission will make a final decision, which in the normal case will be based on the panel's report. The Commission must reach its decision by consensus. If the Commission does not reach its decision expeditiously, and the complainant country feels that it is being injured by the continuing action of the other, it may retaliate with measures of equivalent effect until the matter is resolved.

Dispute resolution under the GATT mechanisms has not proven to be an entirely satisfactory way to resolve international trade disputes. GATT procedures are often extremely lengthy and GATT panel decisions are not binding in their own right. The dispute resolution mechanisms of the FTA are an improvement over the GATT procedures because they provide a faster and more effective forum for dispute avoidance and resolution. Under the GATT, third countries could intervene in a dispute between the United States and Canada, either before a panel or at the time of adoption of the panel decision, complicating and delaying any resolution of the dispute. Futhermore, the offending parties can themselves block adoption of objectionable panel reports, as the United States has done in several agricultural cases involving the European Community. Under the FTA, binational panel rulings in antidumping, countervailing duty, emergency action and certain other cases so designated by the Commission will be binding on the two countries and their agencies.

The establishment of an independent, binational Commission to supervise the operation of the FTA, assist in its further elaboration and resolve disputes is an important achievement in Canada-U.S. trade relations. New formal channels of communication between the two governments, prior to taking any new measures or actions that may affect trade, will be established where there were none before. Also, the express short time limits set out for every stage of consultation, conciliation, arbitration and dispute adjudication should help to ensure that matters are dealt with in an expeditious and efficient manner, at less cost in terms of time and money to affected private firms. The ability of binational panels to make final decisions in antidumping, countervailing duty and emergency action cases, as well as other cases where the Commission directs, should help to provide greater certainty and security of access to the other country's market for Canadian and U.S. exporters.

14

Comparison of Preliminary and Final Texts

Several weeks after the preliminary agreement in principle was signed on October 4, 1987 by Canadian Minister of International Trade, Pat Carney, and U.S. Trade Representative, Clayton Yeutter, the text of the FTA was finally tabled in Parliament and released on December 11. It was delivered to the Prime Minister late the previous evening. There were some changes from the *Preliminary Transcript: Elements of the Agreement*, but, for the most part, they are industry-specific and do not affect the substance of the FTA. The modifications appear to have been made as a result of industry consultations, and most of them enure to Canada's benefit.

APPAREL AND TEXTILES

Significant changes were made in the final text affecting the apparel and textiles industries. The U.S. textiles industry is extremely dissatisfied with the proposed short-term arrangements and has taken its concerns to Congress.

Apparel made wholly from Canadian or U.S. fabrics will qualify for preferential FTA treatment into the United States. For the apparel industry, a tariff-rate quota arrangement will be established such that apparel made in Canada from offshore fabrics will receive preferential

FTA tariff treatment into the United States up to a level of 50 million square yards for non-woolen apparel and 6 million square yards for woolen apparel. The corresponding levels for apparel exported to Canada from the United States will be 10.5 million square yards for non-woolen apparel and 1.1 million square yards for woolen apparel. Above the specified levels, apparel made from offshore fabrics will be liable to pay duty at the Most-Favoured-Nation rates, however, duty drawbacks will be available. For the textile industry, fabrics made in Canada from offshore yarns and exported to the United States will receive preferential FTA tariff treatment up to an annual level of 30 million square yards. The U.S. textile industry will not receive the same benefit. The apparel and textile quotas will be reviewed within two years after the FTA comes into effect and, if not renewed, will expire at the end of 1992.

AUTOMOTIVE TRADE

The provisions affecting automotive trade are clear and should resolve any ambiguities in the *Preliminary Transcript*. There are schedules indicating precisely which companies qualify for preferential treatment under the Auto Pact or other duty waiver and remission programs. Also, there are precise timetables for the phasing out of duty waiver and remission programs for offshore manufacturers. All Canadian and U.S. manufacturers that qualify under the Auto Pact will continue to benefit from duty waivers on vehicles and parts imported into Canada from anywhere in the world. The list of companies that will continue to benefit from Auto Pact safeguards is long and includes the new General Motors-Suzuki joint venture.

FISHERIES

Other changes will benefit the Atlantic fishery. The provincial restrictions on exports of unprocessed fish currently in effect in Quebec, Nova Scotia, New Brunswick, Prince Edward Island and Newfoundland are exempt from the FTA. However, both countries have agreed to retain their rights and obligations under the GATT with respect to existing fish processing restrictions. The British Columbia restrictions, recently the subject of a GATT panel ruling, will be dealt with under the GATT.

PUBLISHING

In a change from the *Preliminary Transcript*, Canada will have no obligation to phase out its differential postal rates for U.S. magazines. However, this may become the subject of a U.S. section 301 action if it is not resolved in the near future.

WINE AND BEER

Existing regulation of beer or other malt-containing beverages will be exempt from the national treatment provisions of the FTA. Special provisions are contained in the final text to ensure that the distribution of locally-produced wine in private retail outlets such as Quebec grocery stores and private stores licensed in Ontario or British Columbia to sell cottage industry wine will be preserved.

ENERGY

Important clarifications have been made in the chapters concerning energy and import and export restrictions. The text makes it abundantly clear that the intent of these chapters is to reaffirm both countries' obligations and commitments under the GATT. The prohibition on the establishment of minimum export-price or import-price requirements for all products, including energy products, is a restatement of the GATT rules. With respect to the regulation of energy exports by the National Energy Board (NEB), the text states that the only price test that the NEB will eliminate is the "least cost alternative test." In what appears to be a modification from the *Preliminary Transcript*, the text indicates that either country may continue to administer a "surplus test." The *Preliminary Transcript* had said that Canada had agreed to limit application of its surplus test to a monitoring function.

The obligation of each country to continue to supply energy products to the other in circumstances of short supply has been clarified. The FTA provides that either country may restrict energy exports for reasons of short supply, conservation of finite resources or national security, but the administration of such restrictions must be fair. In such circumstances, export restrictions may not reduce the proportion of the total export shipments of a specific energy product to the other country relative to the total supply of that product in the exporting country as compared to the proportion prevailing over the last three-year period. It has also been clarified in the investment chapter that the changes in the thresholds for review of U.S. acquisitions of Canadian businesses under the *Investment Canada Act* will not apply to uranium or oil and gas enterprises.

AGRICULTURE

In the chapter relating to agriculture, special conditions have been provided under which the current MFN or pre-FTA tariffs on fresh fruits and vegetables may be re-imposed for temporary periods during and after the end of the transition period. The general provision is that tariffs on fresh fruits and vegetables will be phased out in stages by 1998. However, there is an additional 10-year tariff "snapback" provision for fresh fruits and vegetables. This snapback provision will apply only if the average acreage for a particular product is constant or declining.

INVESTMENT AND SERVICES

In the new areas, such as investment and services, it is clear from the text that the two governments have agreed to proceed cautiously to adopt new international principles. In both chapters, Canada and the United States have expressly provided that subsidy programs, new tax measures and government procurement practices will not be affected by the new obligations and commitments. Also, an important exception has been provided so that the federal governments as well as provincial, state and local governments may continue to regulate for prudential, fiduciary, health and safety or consumer protection reasons.

The investment chapter includes a new provision permitting the imposition of Canadian ownership restrictions where a government-owned enterprise is privatized. This applies to enterprises owned, directly or indirectly, by the federal government, a provincial government or a Crown corporation. It also applies to the subsequent privatization of any business enterprise acquired or established by a government in future.

Cultural industries, transportation services, government procurement and financial services, with the exception of insurance, have been excluded from the investment chapter. The uranium and oil and gas industries will be excluded from the amendments to the *Investment Canada Act* thresholds for review. All existing investment restrictions, with the exception of certain changes to the Investment Canada thresholds for review, have been grandfathered.

In the financial services chapter, an important clarification has been made. The provisions of that chapter will apply only to federally-regulated financial institutions and not to provincially-regulated institutions. This means that provincially-regulated securities firms, trust companies, credit unions and near banks will not be affected by either the financial services chapter or the investment chapter. Therefore, provincial governments will be free to continue regulating financial institutions under their jurisdiction without the influence of the FTA.

The services chapter is both ground-breaking and cautious. It is ground-breaking because the FTA is one of the first international trade agreements to regulate services trade in a comprehensive manner. It is cautious because it applies only to services sectors that did not object to being included. Any sector that expressed reservations about the new regime has been left out. As a result of pressure from the U.S. maritime lobby, the entire transportation industry has been excluded from the services chapter. In the *Preliminary Transcript*, transportation services were to be included in the general services provisions as well as in a specific sectoral agreement. Although designed to appease the U.S. maritime interests, the exclusion of transportation services will also be welcomed by the Canadian trucking industry. The sectoral agreement concerning telecommunications and computer services has been amended to exclude any obligations concerning the establishment or operation of basic telecommunications transport facilities. Financial, legal, health, childcare and government services have also been excluded from the services chapter. The ability of U.S. firms to invest in Canada will be limited by the exceptions in the investment chapter, including those relating to the cultural industries, transportation and financial services.

TRADE REMEDIES

The chapters relating to dispute settlement have been clarified and enhanced. With respect to the antidumping and countervailing duty provisions, private firms involved in a countervailing duty or anti-dumping dispute will be assured access to the new binational panel review procedure. Where a private party notifies its government that it would like to seek binational panel review of a final antidumping or countervailing duty order, the government concerned is required to initiate proceedings on its behalf.

Also, it has been clarified in the FTA that any decision of a binational panel concerning an antidumping or countervailing duty order will be final and binding. A new extraordinary challenge procedure will be established to review binational panel decisions in cases where a member of the panel was guilty of gross misconduct or bias or where the panel manifestly exceeded its powers. This extraordinary procedure was created to deal with the United States' concerns about the integrity of the panel procedure. By agreeing to this new supra-national challenge procedure, Canada has avoided a U.S. request that binational panel decisions be reviewable in the U.S. courts.

It has also been clarified in the text that judicial review of antidumping or countervailing duty decisions will continue to be available to private parties in certain circumstances. For instance, private parties will be able to appeal preliminary decisions made by the relevant agencies, as well as final decisions where neither government has invoked the binational panel procedure, to the courts.

15

Implementation

THE PROCESS

To become fully effective in domestic law, the FTA must be implemented by the Parliament of Canada and the United States Congress. Certain provisions, for example, those providing for changes in listing, pricing and distribution practices relating to wine and distilled liquor, may require implementation by the provincial governments. In the longer term, some of the aspects of the FTA, such as the services and investment obligations, may also require implementation by provincial and state governments.

Under the United States "fast-track" procedures, the text of the FTA and implementing legislation may be introduced in Congress at any time after January 2, 1988. After its introduction, the implementing package will be considered by two Congressional committees, the Senate Finance Committee and the House Ways and Means Committee. Other committees may hold hearings on aspects of the FTA falling within their jurisdiction. In the normal case, each committee will have 45 legislative days in which to report the bill, and each chamber would have 15 legislative days to vote on the bill.

However, the Senate may defer its consideration of the bill until it passes the House and is sent to the Senate. If that happens, a maximum of 90 legislative days would be available for Congress to consider and vote on the implementing legislation. The House has a maximum of sixty legislative days and the Senate has ninety legislative days to consider the implementing bill, and vote "yes" or "no" on it. There is no opportunity for amendments to be made to the FTA or the implementing bill after they have been introduced in Congress. The House and Senate have a straight "yes" or "no" vote. However, there will be extensive consultations among Administration and Congressional officials during the drafting of the implementing legislation.

In Canada, the implementation procedure is less formal. Treaty making, or the negotiation, signing and ratification of an international agreement, is exclusively the responsibility of the federal Crown. It is a constitutional convention, although not law, that international agreements are generally tabled for debate in the House of Commons and the Senate. In many cases, a resolution will be introduced by the government seeking approval of the treaty. Not all international agreements require implementation by the enactment of legislation. Only those treaties which have provisions requiring amendment of existing legislation, the expenditure of public monies or affecting the rights of private citizens need to be implemented by legislation.

Where legislation is required, implementation of specific measures may fall upon the federal Parliament or provincial legislatures, depending upon the subject matter of the measure. If the subject matter is one that falls exclusively within the federal domain, such as provisions relating to tariffs or import and export restrictions, the federal Parliament must enact the implementing legislation. If, on the other hand, the subject matter falls largely within provincial jurisdiction, such as wine and liquor listing, pricing and distribution practices, then the measures concerned should be implemented largely at the provincial level. Implementation, however, also depends on the nature of the regulatory instrument or measure used to govern the practice. Where, for instance, tariff rates are established by Order-in-Council regulation under the Canadian *Customs Act*, they may be changed by the same means. Similarly, provincial wine and liquor practices, promulgated by means of departmental directives and policies, may be changed by similar instruments.

The FTA is, in many respects, an evolutionary document. Many of the obligations and commitments contained in it are forward looking and will not apply to existing government legislation, regulations, practices or measures. Provisions, such as the national treatment obligations relating to trade in services and investment, will require compliance by federal, provincial and state governments when considering new measures that may affect trade in future.

In many areas, such as the antidumping and countervailing duty laws, product standards and technical regulations, financial services, agriculture, government procurement and other service sectors, the two countries have agreed to work together to further liberalize trade in future. The Canada-U.S. Trade Commission will be charged with the responsibility for establishing Working Groups to develop new rules in these areas. Once negotiated, these rules will also require implementation by the appropriate levels of government.

THE TIMETABLE*

October 3, 1987
President Reagan sends notice of intent to sign a trade agreement with Canada to the Congress triggering the fast-track approval process.

October 4, 1987
Elements of Agreement signed by Canadian and U.S. negotiators.

December 10, 1987
Chief negotiators initial legal text of FTA.

December 11, 1987
Tabling of legal text of FTA in the House of Commons.

January 2, 1988
President Reagan and Prime Minister Mulroney sign the FTA.

Spring 1988
Drafting of implementing legislation in Canada and the United States and introduction of legislation in House of Commons and Congress. The FTA and implementing legislation are formally tabled in the U.S. Congress which begins up to 90 "legislative days" for Congress to vote "yes" or "no" to the Agreement and implementing legislation.

January 1, 1989
The FTA and its rules covering such issues as procurement, services, investment and border measures come into effect after both countries exchange Instruments of Ratification. The first round of tariff reductions will begin. For those sectors ready to compete now, tariffs will be eliminated; other goods will begin phasing out their tariffs

---

* Prepared by Government of Canada; revised by the author.

over a five-year or 10-year period. The first tranche will cover about 15 per cent of all goods traded between the two countries including:

Computer and related-equipment	Some pork
Some unprocessed fish	Fur & fur garments
Leather	Whiskey
Yeast	Animal feeds
Unwrought aluminum	Ferro alloys
Vending machines and parts	Needles
Airbrakes for railroad cars	Skis
Skates	Warranty repairs
Some paper-making machinery	Motorcycles

Both nations will end any direct export subsidies to agricultural products going to the other partner. The Canadian embargo on used vehicles imports (those less than 15 years old) from the United States will be lifted in stages. Cars more than eight years old will be allowed entry into Canada duty-free immediately. The age limit will drop about two years every 12 months, until 1994. The Canadian embargo on used aircraft imports will be lifted. Buy-Canadian and Buy-American government procurement policies will be eased.

The Canadian markup difference beyond the cost of service differential on U.S. wine will begin to be phased out. The differential markups on imports of U.S. distilled liquor will be eliminated immediately. The Canadian government will only review direct U.S. takeovers of Canadian companies worth more than $25 million, up from the current $5 million. For indirect takeovers, the threshold for review will be $100 million, up from $50 million. Improved temporary entry for business people is implemented by both countries. U.S. uranium enrichment restrictions are ended.

October 1, 1989
Tariffs on exports to the U.S. of specialty steel products will be lifted in stages.

January 1, 1990
Tariffs will be reduced another fifth or tenth depending upon the schedule.

January 1, 1991
Canadian foreign investment review for direct takeovers rises to $100 million; for indirect takeovers, $500 million. Tariffs will continue

to be reduced; the 35 per cent U.S. duty on Canadian shakes and shingles is scheduled to come off.

January 1, 1992

The threshold for Canadian foreign investment review increases to $150 million; indirect takeovers will no longer be scrutinized. Tariff reductions continue.

January 1, 1993

Tariffs will have been lifted on another 35 per cent of dutiable goods, including:

Subway cars	Chemicals including resins
Printed matter	(excluding drugs and
Paper and paper products	cosmetics)
Paints	Furniture
Explosives	Hardwood plywood
Telecommunications equipment	Aftermarket auto parts
Most machinery	Some meats (including
	lamb)

The Canadian embargo on the import of used cars ends, as does the U.S. embargo on the importation of lottery materials.

January 1, 1994

U.S. customs user fees and duty drawbacks for other countries will end. U.S. foreign trade zone provisions will change to Canada's benefit. New regime on countervailing duty and antidumping laws should come into effect.

January 1, 1995

Tariffs are reduced further.

January 1, 1996

There will be another tariff cut. This is the final deadline for Canada and the United States to agree on new trade remedy laws. Production-based duty waivers for production in the auto industry will end.

January 1, 1997

Another tariff reduction.

January 1, 1998

Tariffs will have been eliminated on remaining goods:

Most agricultural products	Steel
Textiles and apparel	Appliances
Softwood plywood	Beef
Pleasure craft	Tires

The tariff snapback provisions for vegetables and fresh fruits will remain for another decade.

16

The Omnibus Trade Bill

The U.S. House of Representatives and Senate have passed different versions of H.R. 3, the 1987 Omnibus Trade Bill. It is currently in the process of being reconciled by a bipartisan House-Senate conference committee. Some of the steam was taken out of the bill as a result of the crisis in financial markets and other pressing domestic policy concerns in 1987, but it is prominent on the Congressional agenda in 1988. Some observers have expressed concern about the Omnibus Trade Bill and the FTA package being introduced in Congress around the same time. The Administration has considerable discretion as to when it will submit the FTA and implementing legislation to Congress. If it is submitted too early, there is a risk that Congress may try to extract concessions from the President regarding the trade bill in return for approval of the FTA. The timing of submission of the FTA package and passage of the trade bill are critical and could have major consequences for Canada.

There is some controversy about whether the provisions of the Omnibus Trade Bill will apply to Canada. The legislative watchdog procedures in the FTA will not apply to a trade bill enacted in 1988 because the FTA does not come into effect until January 1, 1989. Accompanying letters to the FTA provide a standstill understanding that both countries "understand the need to exercise their discretion in the period prior to entry into force so as not to jeopardize the approval process or undermine the spirit and mutual benefits of the Free Trade Agreement." It is the view of some Canadian observers, including Ambassador Simon Reisman, that the enactment by the United States of a major trade bill similar to the Senate and House versions of H.R. 3 would constitute an impairment of the benefits and objectives of the FTA.

If it wished to, Congress could explicitly exempt Canada from the provisions of the Omnibus Trade Bill. The House version of H.R. 3 establishes such a precedent for any bilateral free trade area agreement that came into force before January 1, 1987. It provides that if there is any inconsistency between any provisions of the Omnibus Trade Bill and such a free trade area agreement, the provisions of the trade bill will not apply to that country. Presumably, an amendment could be made to the Omnibus Trade Bill exempting Canada from its provisions.

The current versions of H.R. 3 contain extensive changes to the U.S. trade laws which could have significant implications for Canadian industries. The cumulative effect of the bill will be to make it much easier for U.S. petitioners to obtain import relief, thereby increasing the harassment of Canadian and other foreign firms under the U.S. trade laws.

ANTIDUMPING AND COUNTERVAILING DUTY LAWS

Many changes are proposed that would significantly increase the opportunities for the application and enforcement of the antidumping and countervailing duty laws. The House bill contains amendments to the Antidumping Act of 1916 that would place the burden of proof on foreign exporters to establish that there was no intention to injure a U.S. domestic industry. This provision would encourage U.S. industries to bring private antidumping cases in the courts.

Both the House and Senate versions would revise the definition of subsidy in the U.S. countervailing duty law to codify the 1986 Department of Commerce preliminary determination in *Certain Softwood Lumber Products from Canada*. By extending the definition of "specificity", this proposed amendment would enable U.S. industries to attack a wide variety of industrial targeting practices of foreign governments. Many of the proposed changes, such as the provisions relating to multiple-offender monitoring, downstream product monitoring, diversionary input dumping, "sham transactions", and circumvention, would expand the scope of antidumping or countervailing duty investigations and permit an order made in a particular case to apply to a wider range of products and persons.

Both versions would also make it easier to establish material injury by limiting the injury inquiry to domestic producers with production facilities within the United States. Legislative proposals would specifically require cross-cumulation of findings in antidumping and countervailing duty investigations in determining injury. Also, both bills would include such unfair trade considerations as antidumping orders made in other countries and the impact of dumped or subsidized imports on research and development plans in an injury investigation.

SECTION 301

Significant changes to section 301 of the Trade Act of 1974 are proposed in the Omnibus Trade Bill. Currently, section 301 allows private industries to petition the President to seek remedies for certain acts, policies or practices of a foreign government that adversely affect U.S. commerce in goods, services or trade-related investment. Unlike the antidumping and countervailing duty laws, section 301 is not directed primarily at providing U.S. industries with relief against foreign import competition. It is intended to remedy foreign government practices that inhibit or restrict the competitiveness of U.S. firms in foreign and domestic markets. Both bills would transfer authority from the President to the United States Trade Representative ("USTR") to determine whether a particular foreign government act, policy or practice is inconsistent with a trade agreement or unjustifiable unreasonable and a burden on U.S. commerce.

Both versions would provide for mandatory retaliation in certain cases. The Senate bill would require mandatory self-initiation of an investigation in cases where expansion of U.S. trade is most likely and against countries maintaining a consistent pattern of import barriers, such as Japan. Both bills explicitly define which acts may be considered actionable and add a new category of actionable practices, that of "export targeting". Foreign government policies or practices which deny national treatment to U.S. goods, services or investment are deemed in the Senate version to be actionable. H.R. 3 would provide shorter time periods for determinations and decisions to take action, particularly in cases involving export targeting.

Section 301 may be described as the wild card in the deck of the U.S. trade laws. These bills constitute a significant break with past tradition. By limiting Presidential discretion and requiring mandatory retaliation in certain circumstances, Congress is attempting to change section 301 from a mechanism for facilitating international dispute settlement to a responsive, administrative procedure designed to protect and promote U.S. industries. Although it is difficult to predict exactly what will emerge from the committee conference, the Omnibus Trade Bill will almost certainly broaden the scope for action and expand the list of actionable foreign government practices under section 301. With more formalized administrative procedures and shorter time deadlines, it can reasonably be expected that more investigations will be initiated and retaliatory action will be taken in more cases. This is likely to exacerbate international trade relations and could lead to retaliation by foreign countries.

SECTION 337 — UNFAIR TRADE

The proposed legislation would also make section 337 of the Tariff Act of 1930 a more ready, effective import relief remedy for U.S. industries. Section 337 currently authorizes the U.S. International Trade Commission ("ITC") to exclude from entry into the United States imported products tainted with unfair trade practices, such as violations of the intellectual property or antitrust laws, where those practices injure an efficiently and economically-operated U.S. industry. The ITC can also order the persons or companies responsible for these unfair acts to cease and desist from those acts.

Section 337 is currently a speedy, summary remedy for U.S. industries. The ITC is required to complete its investigation within one year, or 18 months in more complicated cases. As a result, actions brought under section 337 are dealt with more expeditiously than court actions. Both the House and Senate bills contain amendments to eliminate the injury requirement in cases involving intellectual property rights. In addition, both bills would substantially expand the definition of what constitutes a U.S. industry. The House version proposes to expand the definition of intellectual property to include trade secrets ad common law trade marks as well as registered patents, trade marks and copyrights. These proposed amendments would make section 337 an even more expeditious and effective import relief measure for U.S. petitioners.

SECTION 201 — ESCAPE CLAUSE

The Omnibus Trade Bill would amend section 201 of the Trade Act of 1974 by easing the requirements to prove injury, limiting Presidential discretion in imposing import relief and expanding the provisions for industrial adjustment. Under section 201, the U.S. escape clause or safeguards law, the President can impose import restrictions where there has been a sudden increase in imports that cause serious injury or a threat thereof to a domestic industry. Both bills would instruct the ITC to consider more factors in its determination of serious injury. The Senate bill, in particular, would require the ITC to consider antidumping or countervailing duty orders relating to the same product, difficulties of the domestic industry in maintaining research and development expenditures, and foreign export targeting practices. The Senate version would limit Presidential discretion by requiring him to provide the equivalent of import relief recommended by the ITC unless there would be serious economic harm caused by such action.

CONCLUSION

It is difficult to predict exactly what form the 1988 Omnibus Trade Bill will take. There is a very strong constituency in Congress for passing a comprehensive trade reform bill in this election year. The Administration has indicated that it will veto a bill that is largely protectionist in nature. Whatever the outcome, it is certain that any trade bill enacted in 1988 will contain comprehensive changes to the U.S. trade laws. The cumulative effect of these changes will be to expand the opportunities for U.S. industries to obtain import relief and to increase the harassment and uncertainty experienced by foreign, including Canadian, exporters.

The timing of Congressional consideration of the Omnibus Trade Bill and the FTA implementing package will be delicate and critical for Canadian exporters. In a recent exchange of letters between Congressional leaders and the Administration, the Administration agreed to defer introduction of the FTA package until June 1988, and the Congressional leaders agreed to vote on the implementing legislation expeditiously.

On behalf of the government of Canada, Ambassador Gotlieb has asked Congressional leaders for an exemption for Canada from the provisions of the Omnibus Trade Bill. If Canada does not receive special treatment in the U.S. trade legislation, there are likely to be significant implications for the implementation of the FTA. Several observers, including the Honourable Donald Macdonald and Ambassador Simon Reisman, as well as the House of Commons Standing Committee on External Affairs and International Trade, have recommended that Canada should consider the FTA at an end if a U.S. trade bill is enacted containing seriously protectionist measures affecting Canada.

Directory

The International Trade Communications Group, Department of External Affairs, maintains a toll-free telephone line to answer inquiries about the Free Trade Agreement (1-800-387-0660). Copies of the full text of the Agreement along with official background documents may be ordered free of charge by telephone or obtained from offices of the Federal Business Development Bank and the Department of Regional Industrial Expansion, at any of the addresses listed below.

Free copies of the Agreement are also available at Carswell display centres in Toronto, Calgary and Vancouver.

DISPLAY CENTRES

Toronto
120 York St.
Toronto, Ont.

Calgary
800 Rocky Mountain Plaza
615 Macleod Trail S.E.
Calgary, Alberta

Vancouver
815 West Hastings St.
Vancouver, B.C.

DRIE OFFICES

Ms. Joan Enman
Bentall Tower IV
1101 - 1055 Dunsmuir Street
P.O. Box 49178
Vancouver, British Columbia
V7X 1K8

Mr. Ron Selin
The Cornerpoint Building
10179 - 105th Street, Suite 505
Edmonton, Alberta
T5J 3S3

DRIE OFFICES — *continued*
Mr. Brian Beattie
6th Floor
105 - 21st Street, East
Saskatcoon, Saskatchewan
S7K 0B3

Ms. Joanne Spanton
Trade and Industrial Officer
608 - 330 Portage Avenue
P.O. Box 981
Winnipeg, Manitoba
R3C 2V2

Ms. Marie Fortin Balogh
Director General
Trade and Business Development
1 First Canadian Place
Suite 484
P.O. Box 98
Toronto, Ontario
M5X 1B1

Mme Celine Seguin
International Trade Development
800, Place Victoria, 38e étage
C.P. 247
Montréal, Québec
H4Z 1E8

Mr. Gordon MacLennon
770 Main Street, 14th Floor
P.O. Box 1210
Moncton, New Brunswick
E1C 8P9

Ms. Winnifred Desjardins
P.O. Box 940, Postal Station "M"
Halifax, Nova Scotia
B3J 2V9

Mr. Chris Wells
134 Kent Street
P.O. Box 1115
Charlottetown, P.E.I.
C1A 7M8

Mr. Ed Coady
Investment and Technology
90 O'Leary Avenue
P.O. Box 8950
St. John's, Newfoundland
A1B 3R9

Mr. Larry Bagnell
Director
301 -108 Lambert Street
Whitehorse, Yukon
Y1A 1Z2

Mr. Jeff Titterington
P.O. Box 6100
Yellowknife, Northwest Territories
X1A 1C0

FBDB OFFICES

Scotia Square
Cogswell Tower
Suite 1400
Scotia Square
P.O. Box 1656
Halifax, Nova Scotia
B3J 2Z7

Herald Tower
4 Heard Avenue
P.O. Box 790
Corner Brook, Newfoundland
A2H 6G7

42 High-Street
P.O. Box 744
Grand Falls, Newfoundland
A2A 2M4

4th Floor
Atlantic Place
215 Water Street
P.O. Box 520
Postal Station "C"
St. John's Newfoundland
A1C 5K4

FBDB OFFICES — *continued*
448 King Street
P.O. Box 540
Bridgewater, Nova Scotia
B4V 1A9

48-50 Dorchester Street
P.O. Box 726
Sydney, Nova Scotia
B1P 6H7

802 Prince Street
Suite 202
P.O. Box 1378
Truro, Nova Scotia
B2N 5N2

270 Douglas Avenue
5th Floor
P.O. Box 780
Bathurst, New Brunswick
E2A 4A5

121 de l'Eglise Street
Suite 401
P.O. Box 610
Edmundston, New Brunswick
E3V 3L2

King's Place Complex
Suite 644 - 440 King Street
P.O. Box 1235
Fredericton, New Brunswick
E3B 5H8

860 Main Street
7th Floor
P.O. Box 1090
Moncton, New Brunswick
E1C 1G2

75 Prince William Street
P.O. Box 7173
Postal Station "A"
Saint John, New Brunswick
E2L 4S6

180 Kent Street
3rd Floor
P.O. Box 488
Charlottetown, P.E.I.
C1A 1N9

800 Victoria Square
Place Victoria
Suite 4600
P.O. Box 190
Montreal, Quebec
H4Z 1C8

475 rue des Champs Elysées
Chicoutimi, Quebec
G7H 5V7

1010 des Galeries
Drummondville, Quebec
J2C 5W4

161 rue Principale
Granby, Quebec
J2G 2V5

Plaza Val Tétreau
400 boul. Alexandre-Taché
Hull, Quebec
J9A 1M5

2525 boul. Daniel-Johnson
Chomedey, Laval, Quebec
H7T 1S9

550 Chemin Chambly, Suite 100
Longueuil, Quebec
J4H 3L8

800 Victoria Square
Place Victoria
Ground Floor
P.O. Box 187
Montreal, Quebec
H4Z 1C8

FBDB OFFICES — *continued*
6068 rue Sherbrooke est
Montreal, Quebec
H1N 1C1

871 Chemin St-Louis
Québec, Quebec
G1S 1C1

320 rue St-Germain est
Suite 702
Rimouski, Quebec
G5L 1C2

147 avenue Mercier
Rouyn, Quebec
J9X 4X4

500 boul. des Laurentides
Suite 230
Galeries des Laurentides
St-Antoine des Laurentides, Quebec
J7Z 4M2

3100 Côte Vertu
Suite 160
St-Laurent, Quebec
H4R 2J8

106 rue-LNapoléon
Suite 305
Sept-Iles, Quebec
G4R 3L7

2532 rue King ouest
Sherbrooke, Quebec
J1J 2E8

1410 rue des Cyprès
Trois-Rivières, Quebec
G8Y 4S3

777 Bay Street
29th Floor
Toronto, Ontario
M5G 2C8

151 Dunlop Street East
P.O. Box 876
Barrie, Ontario
L4M 4Y6

8 Main Street East
P.O. Box 619
Hamilton, Ontario
L8N 1E8

20 Main Street South
Kenora, Ontario
P9N 1S7

Plaza 16
16 Bath Road
Kingston, Ontario
K7L 1H4

Commerce House
50 Queen Street North
4th Floor
P.O. Box 2667
Postal Station "B"
Kitchener, Ontario
N2H 6N2

197 York Street
Suite 1000
London, Ontario
N6A 1B2

33 City Centre Drive
Suite 145
Square One, Northern Telecom
    Building
Mississauga, Ontario
L5B 2N5

205 Main Street East
P.O. Box 925
North Bay, Ontario
P1B 8K1

22 King Street West
5th Floor
Oshawa, Ontario
L1H 1A3

FBDB OFFICES — *continued*
280 Albert Street
Ottawa, Ontario
K1P 5G8

340 George Street North
P.O. Box 1419
Peterbrough, Ontario
K9H 7H6

43 Church Street
Suite 504
P.O. Box 1193
St. Catharines, Ontario
L2R 7A7

405 Queen Street East
Sault Ste. Marie, Ontario
P6A 1Z5

Canada Life Centre
Suite 516
55 Town Centre Court
Scarborough, Ontario
M1P 4X4

1036 Ontario Street
Stratford, Ontario
N5A 6Z3

1 Elm Street
P.O. Box 820
Sudbury, Ontario
P3C 1R6

905 Victoria Avenue East
P.O. Box 878
Station "F"
Thunder Bay, Ontario
P7C 4X7

83 Algonquin Blvd. West
P.O. Box 1240
Timmins, Ontario
P4N 2R4

777 Bay Street
29th floor
Toronto, Ontario
M5G 2C8

7501 Keele Street
Suite 200
Concord, Ontario
L4K 1Y2

500 Ouellette Avenue
Windsor, Ontario
N9A 1B3

155 Carleton St.
Suite 1200
Winnipeg, Manitoba
R3C 3H8

940 Princess Avenue
Brandon, Manitoba
R7A 0P6

386 Broadway Avenue
Suites 101 & 105
Winnipeg, Manitoba
R3C 3R6

Bank of Canada Bldg.
Suite 320
2220 - 12th Avenue
Regina, Saskatchewan
S4P 0M8

8th Floor, Canada Bldg.
105 - 21st Street East
Saskatoon, Saskatchewan
S7K 0B3

3015 - 12th Street N.E.
Suite 170
Calgary, Alberta
T2E 7J2

FBDB OFFICES — *continued*
606 Principal Plaza
10303 Jasper Avenue
Edmonton, Alberta
T5J 3N6

10135 - 101st Avenue
P.O. Box 10
Grande Prairie, Alberta
T8V 0Y4

Professional Building
Suite 500
740 -4th Aveune South
Lethbridge, Alberta
T1J 0N9

Riverside Office Plaza
Suite 100
4919 - 59th Street
Red Deer, Alberta
T4N 6C9

Scotia Centre
Suite 203
5102 Franklin Avenue
P.O. Box 70
Yellowknife, N.W.T.
X1A 2N1

900 West Hastings Street
Vancouver, British Columbia
V6C 1E7

1260 Island Highway
Campbell River, British Columbia
V9W 2C8

30 South 11th Avenue
Cranbrook, British Columbia
V1C 2P1

9900 - 100th Avenue
Suite 315
Fort St. John, British Columbia
V1J 5S7

63 West Victoria
Suite 100
Kamloops, British Columbia
V2C 6L3

260 Harvey Avenue
Kelowna, British Columbia
V1Y 7S5

20316 - 56th Avenue #101
Langley, British Columbia
V3A 3Y7

190 Wallace Street
Nanaimo, British Columbia
V9R 5B1

227 - 6th Street
New Westminister, British Columbia
V3L 3A5

6-221 West Esplanade
North Vancouver, British Columbia
V7M 3J3

299 Victoria Street
Suite 200
Prince George, British Columbia
V2L 5B8

4641 Lazelle Avenue
Terrace, British Columbia
V8G 1S8

3303 - 30th Street
Vernon, British Columbia
V1T 5E4

990 Fort Street
Victoria, British Columbia
V8V 3K2

94 North First Avenue
Williams Lake, British Columbia
V2G 1Y6

240-204 Lambert Street
Whitehorse, Yukon Territory
Y1A 1Z4

Glossary of Trade and Related Terms*

International trade, like other specialized fields, has its own distinctive vocabulary which mystifies laymen — even experts. Many non-specialists stumble over terms commonly used in trade negotiations such as the acronyms that represent international organizations that guide, regulate, and facilitate trade, or Canadian and U.S. departments and agencies responsible for trade policy. This glossary provides a guide to many of the specialized terms, abbreviations and acronyms used in international trade negotiations.

The definitions included in this glossary are drawn or adapted from a variety of sources, the most important of which is a glossary prepared by the United States Department of Commerce.

ACTN Advisory Committee on Trade Negotiations. Principal forum for U.S. business to advise U.S. Trade Representative on bilateral or multilateral trade negotiations.

Adjustment The ongoing process by which the economy declines or renews and adjusts to changing circumstances. Among the factors that influence the scope and pace of adjustment are changes in technology and productivity, trade liberalization, consumer tastes, resource exhaustion, and the changing composition of the labour force. See also structural change.

Adjustment Assistance Financial, training and reemployment technical assistance to workers and technical assistance to firms and industries to help them cope with adjustment difficulties arising

---

*Originally published by Government of Canada; revised and abridged by the author.

from increased import competition. The objective of the assistance is usually to help an industry to become more competitive in the same line of production, or to move into other economic activities. The aid to workers can take the form of training (to qualify the affected individuals for employment in new or expanding industries), relocation allowances (to help them move from areas characterized by high unemployment to areas where employment may be available) or unemployment compensation (to tide them over while they are searching for new jobs). The benefits of increased trade to an importing country generally exceed the costs of adjustment, but the benefits are widely shared and the adjustment costs are sometimes concentrated on a few domestic producers and communities. Both import restraints and adjustment assistance can be designed to reduce these hardships but adjustment assistance, unlike import restraints, allows the economy to enjoy the full benefits of lower-cost, imported goods. Adjustment assistance can also be designed to facilitate structural shifts of resources from less productive to more productive industries, contributing to greater economic efficiency and an improved standard of living.

Ad Valorem Tariff   A tariff calculated as a percentage of the value of goods cleared through Customs, e.g. 15 per cent ad valorem means 15 percent of the value.

Agreement on Technical Barriers to Trade (Product Standards Code)   A code of conduct negotiated under the auspices of the GATT during the Tokyo Round of the MTN that established substantive rules for the imposition of technical or product standards and procedures for product testing and certification.

Antidumping Code   A code of conduct negotiated under the auspices of GATT during the Kennedy and Tokyo Rounds of the MTN that established substantive and procedural standards for domestic and multilateral antidumping proceedings. See also Code of Conduct and Dumping.

Antidumping Duties   Additional duties imposed by an importing country in circumstances where imports are priced at less than the "normal" price charged in the exporter's domestic market and are causing material injury to a domestic industry in the importing country.

Auto Pact   A sectoral trade agreement, the Agreement Concerning Automotive Products Between the Government of the United States and the Government of Canada, entered into in 1965 in order to encourage the rationalization and growth of the North American auto industry. It provides for duty-free movement between the two countries of new automobiles and original equipment parts. In the case of Canada, producers who qualify are allowed to import automobiles and parts duty-free from anywhere in the world.

Balance of Payments   A tabulation of a country's credit and debit transactions with other countries and international institutions. These transactions are divided into two broad groups: Current Account and Capital Account. The Current Account includes exports and imports of goods, services (including investment income), and unilateral transfers. The Capital Account includes financial flows related to international direct investment, investment in government and private securities, international bank transactions, and changes in official gold holdings and foreign exchange reserves.

Balance of Trade   A component of the balance of payments (the surplus or the deficit) that results from comparing a country's expenditures on merchandise imports and receipts derived from its merchandise exports.

Barter   The direct exchange of goods for other goods, without the use of money as a medium of exchange and without the involvement of a third party.

Beggar-Thy-Neighbor Policy   A course of action through which a country tries to reduce unemployment and increase domestic output by raising tariffs and establishing non-tariff barriers that impede imports, or accomplishes the same objective through competitive devaluation. Countries that pursued such policies in the early 1930s found that other countries retaliated by raising their own barriers against imports, which, by reducing export markets, tended to worsen the economic difficulties that precipitated the initial protectionist actions. The U.S. Smoot-Hawley Tariff Act of 1930 is often cited as an example of this approach.

Berne Convention   International agreement providing for national treatment in the protection of intellectual property. Together with the Paris Convention, it provides the basis for the multilateral intellectual property regime administered by WIPO.

Bilateral Trade Agreement   A formal or informal agreement involving commerce between two countries. Such agreements sometimes list the quantities of specific goods that may be exchanged between participating countries within a given period.

Binding Arbitration Concept in dispute settlement where the parties to the dispute agree at the outset that they and their agencies will abide by the results of dispute settlement procedures.

Border Tax Adjustments The remission of taxes on exported goods, including sales taxes and value-added taxes, designed to ensure that national tax systems do not impede exports. The GATT permits such frontier adjustments on exports for indirect taxes on the condition that these are passed on to consumers, but not for direct taxes (e.g., income taxes assessed on producing firms).

Bounties or Grants Payments by governments to producers of goods, often to strengthen their competitive position. See also subsidies.

Boycott A refusal to deal commercially or otherwise with a person, firm or country.

Buy National Discriminatory government procurement policies, such as Buy America or Buy Canadian policies, which provide a margin of preference for local suppliers over foreign suppliers. The GATT does not require non-discrimination by governments in all of their purchasing policies. The Government Procurement Code, agreed to during the Tokyo Round, provides for non-discriminatory purchasing practices by specified government entities. See Government Procurement Code.

Capital Account In the calculation of the balance of payments, the Capital Account includes financial flows related to international direct investment, investment in government and private securities, international bank transactions, and changes in official gold holdings and foreign exchange reserves.

CIF An abbreviation used in some international sales contracts, where the selling price includes all "costs, insurance and freight" for the goods sold ("charged in full"), meaning that the seller arranges and pays for all relevant expenses involved in shipping goods from their point of exportation to a given point of importation. In import statistics, "CIF value" means that all figures are calculated on this basis, regardless of the nature of individual transactions.

CIT Canadian Import Tribunal, a body responsible under Canadian legislation for findings of injury in antidumping and countervailing duty cases, and the provision of advice to the government on other import issues.

CIT U.S. Court of International Trade; special court set up in the U.S. to hear appeals from administrative and quasi-judicial trade decisions, e.g., from decisions of the ITC or ITA.

COCOM Coordinating Committee responsible for the international coordination of export controls on strategic material and products from restricted countries. Members include U.S.A., Canada, UK, France, Italy, Belgium, Japan, Denmark, Germany (FR), Netherlands, Norway, Greece, Portugal, and Turkey.

Code of Conduct Several codes of conduct were negotiated during the Tokyo Round of MTN to reduce non-tariff barriers, or domestic measures that impede trade. These are considered legally binding for the countries that choose to adhere to them. Each of these codes is monitored by a special committee that meets under the auspices of GATT and encourages consultations and the settlement of disputes arising under the specific code. Countries that are not Contracting Parties to GATT may be signatories to these codes. Also, not all Contracting Parties to the GATT are signatories to each code. GATT Articles III through XXIII also contain commercial policy provisions that have been described as GATT's code of good conduct in trade matters. The United Nations has also encouraged the negotiation of several "voluntary" codes of conduct, including one that seeks to specify the rights and obligations of trans-national corporations and of governments.

Commercial Presence Trade in services principle; establishing the corporate presence that a national or enterprise of one country requires in order to carry out a service transaction, such as a branch or agency office, in another country. This principle falls short of a right of establishment.

Commodity Broadly defined, any article exchanged in trade, but most commonly used to refer to raw materials, including such minerals as tin, copper and manganese, and bulk-produced agricultural products such as coffee, tea and rubber.

Commodity Agreement An international understanding, formally accepted by the principal exporters and importers, regarding international trading of a raw material and usually intended to affect its price. Some producing countries would like to use commodity agreements to raise prices for the commodities they produce. Consuming countries generally are willing to agree only to commodity agreements that seek to moderate extreme price fluctuations.

Common External Tariff (CXT) A tariff rate uniformly applied by a common market or customs union, such as the European Community, to imports from countries outside the union. For example, the European Common Market is based on the principle of a free internal trade area with a common external tariff. Free trade areas, by definition, do not have common external tariffs. Members of an FTA each retain their own respective tariff schedules vis-à-vis third countries.

Comparative Advantage A central concept in international trade theory which holds that a country or a region should specialize in the production and export of those goods and services that it can produce more efficiently than other goods and services, and import those goods and services in which it has a comparative disadvantage. This theory was first propounded by David Ricardo in 1817 as a basis for increasing the economic welfare of a population through international trade. The comparative advantage theory normally favours specialized production in a country based on intensive utilization of those factors of production in which the country is relatively well-endowed (such as raw materials, fertile land, skilled labor), the accumulation of physical capital or research and development expertise.

Compensation Concept that withdrawal or amendment of a previously negotiated or bound concession, such as a tariff increase, change in quota level, temporary surtax etc., requires a new and equivalent concession.

Countertrade Transactions in which the seller provides the buyer with deliveries (e.g., technology, know-how, finished products, machinery and equipment) and contractually agrees to purchase goods from the buyer equal to an agreed-upon percentage of the original sales contract value. A practice which has become increasingly prevalent in East-West trade: nonmarket economy countries have adopted countertrade in various forms as a tool for generating some or all of the hard currency needed for new industrial projects, expanding exports to the West and minimizing the outlay of scarce resources of hard currency. Also referred to as barter, buy back, counterpurchase, offset and compensation trade.

Countervailing Duties Additional duties imposed by an importing country to offset government subsidies in an exporting country, when subsidized imports cause material injury to a domestic industry in the importing country.

Current Account That portion of a country's balance of payments that records current (as opposed to capital) transactions, including visible trade (exports and imports), invisible trade (income and expenditures for services), profits earned from foreign operations, interest and transfer payments.

Customs Act   Canadian legislation which provides the basic framework for customs classification and valuation procedures in Canada.

Customs Classification   The particular category in a tariff nomenclature in which a product is classified for tariff purposes, or the procedure for determining the appropriate tariff category in a country's nomenclature system used for the classification, coding and description of internationally traded goods. Most important trading nations — except for the United States and the Soviet Union — classify imported goods in conformity with the Customs Cooperation Council Nomenclature (CCCN), formerly known as the Brussels Tariff Nomenclature (BTN). The United States is expected to adopt this nomenclature in 1988.

Customs Cooperation Council Nomenclature (CCCN)   See Harmonized System.

Customs Duties   See Tariff.

Customs Harmonization   International efforts to increase the uniformity of customs nomenclatures and procedures in cooperating countries. The Customs Cooperation Council has been seeking, since 1970, to develop an up-to-date and internationally accepted "Harmonized Commodity Coding and Description System" for classifying goods for customs, statistical, and other purposes. See also Kyoto Convention.

Customs Tariff   Canadian legislation which provides the legal framework for the collection of customs duties in Canada, including rules related to drawbacks, duty remission, tariff rates, etc.

Defence Production Sharing Arrangements   A set of administrative arrangements between the United States and Canada dating back to the 1941 Hyde Park Arrangement providing for free trade in defence material and encouraging shared production of such material.

Devaluation   The lowering of the value of a national currency in terms of the currency of another nation. Devaluation tends to reduce domestic demand for imports in a country by raising import prices in terms of the devalued currency, and to raise foreign demand for the country's exports by reducing export prices in terms of foreign currencies. Devaluation can therefore help to correct a balance of payments deficit and sometimes provides a short-term basis for economic adjustment of a national economy.

Developed Countries   A term to distinguish the more industrialized nations, including all OECD member countries as well as the Soviet Union and most of the socialist countries of Eastern Europe, — from "developing" or "less developed" countries. The developed countries are sometimes collectively designated as the "North," because most of them are in the northern hemisphere.

Developing Countries   A broad range of countries that generally lack a high degree of industrialization, infrastructure and other capital investment, sophisticated technology, widespread literacy, and advanced living standards among their populations as a whole. The developing countries are sometimes collectively designated as the "South" because a large number of them are in the southern hemisphere.

Dispute Settlement   Those institutional provisions in an international trade agreement which provide the means by which differences or disputes between the parties can be avoided or settled.

Domestic Content Requirements   A requirement that firms selling a particular product within a particular country must use, as a certain percentage of their inputs, goods produced within or originating from that country.

Dumping   The sale of an imported good at a price lower than that at which it is sold within the exporting country or to third countries. Dumping is generally recognized as an unfair trade practice that can disrupt markets and injure producers of competitive products in an importing country. Article VI of GATT and the Antidumping Code permit the imposition of antidumping duties against "dumped" imported goods equal to the difference between their export price and their normal value in the exporting country.

Duty   See Tariff.

Duty Remission   Import duties or taxes waived or remitted by a government, in whole or in part, to a particular company or industry contingent upon exports manufactured in the importing country or similar performance requirements, usually on imports of components, parts or products to complete a product line.

Drawback   Import duties or taxes repaid by a government in whole or in part, when the imported goods are re-exported or used in the manufacture of exported goods.

EEC   European Economic Community, comprising, as of January 1, 1986, France, Italy, Belgium, Germany (FR), Netherlands, Luxembourg, Denmark, UK, Ireland, Greece, Spain and Portugal.

EFTA European Free Trade Area, comprising Austria, Switzerland, Finland, Iceland, Norway and Sweden.

Embargo A prohibition upon exports or imports, either with respect to specific products or specific countries. Historically, embargoes have been ordered most frequently in time of war, but they may also be applied for political, economic or sanitary purposes. Embargoes imposed against an individual country by the United Nations, or a group of nations, in an effort to influence its conduct or its policies are sometimes called "sanctions".

Emergency Actions See Escape Clause, Safeguards, and Section 201.

End-use Tariff Item Tariff classification where the rate of duty depends upon the use to which the imported product is put, e.g. cotton sheeting for medical use is taxed at a lower rate than other cotton sheeting.

Escape Clause A provision in a bilateral or multilateral commercial agreement permitting a signatory nation to impose duties or other restrictions when increasing imports cause serious harm to the producers of competitive domestic goods. GATT Article XIX permits such "safeguards" to help firms and workers adversely affected by a sudden surge of imports adjust to the rising level of import competition. See also Safeguards.

Establishment, Right of One of the basic principles for liberalization of investment. Right of establishment involves providing foreign investors with the right to establish new businesses or acquire existing ones on the same basis as nationals.

Exceptions Provisions in a trade agreement which provide rules to deal with special circumstances, such as import or export controls for security reasons. GATT Articles XX and XXI provide for the basic exceptions to the GATT.

Exchange Controls The rationing of foreign currencies, bank drafts, and other instruments for settling international financial obligations by countries seeking to ameliorate acute balance of payments difficulties. When such measures are imposed, importers must apply for prior authorization from the government to obtain the foreign currency required to bring in designated amounts and types of goods. Since such measures have the effect of restricting imports, they are considered non-tariff barriers to trade.

Exchange Rate The price (or rate) at which one currency is exchanged for another currency, for gold, or for Special Drawing Rights (SDR's).

Excise Tax   A selective tax, sometimes called a consumption tax, on certain goods produced within or imported into a country.

Exemptions   Provisions which exempt particular products or situations from a general rule, e.g., in a free-trade area eliminating all tariffs, agricultural products might be exempted.

Export and Import Permits Act   Canadian legislation which provides a licensing mechanism by which exports from Canada and imports into Canada can be controlled. Three basic lists are prescribed under the Act: an Import Control List, an Export Control List, and an Area Control List. Any product listed on the first two lists or any exports to a country on the third list requires a permit. The conditions are prescribed by Order-in-Council. The Act also provides the Canadian legislative authority for Escape Clause or Safeguards Actions.

Export Quotas   Quantitive restrictions or ceilings imposed by an exporting country on the value or volume of certain products. Some International Commodity Agreements explicitly indicate when countries should apply such restraints. Export Quotas are also often applied in Orderly Marketing Agreements and Voluntary Restraint Agreements, and to promote domestic processing of raw materials in countries that produce them.

Export Restraints   Quantitative restrictions imposed by exporting countries to limit exports to specified foreign markets, usually pursuant to a formal or informal agreement concluded at the request of the importing countries, such as an OMA or VRA.

Export Subsidies   Government payments or other financial benefits provided to domestic producers or exporters contingent on the export of their goods or services. GATT Article XVI recognizes that subsidies in general, and especially export subsidies, may have trade-distorting effects and hinder the achievement of GATT objectives. An Agreement on Subsidies and Countervailing Duties (the "Subsidies Code") negotiated during the Tokyo Round provided for an outright prohibition of export subsidies by developed countries for manufactured and semi-manufactured products. The Code also established a special committee, serviced by signatories. Under certain conditions, the Code allows developing countries to use export subsidies on manufactured and semi-manufactured products, and all countries to use export subsidies on primary products, including agricultural products, provided that the subsidies do not result in a country obtaining a more than equitable share of world exports.

Export Trading Company A corporation or other business entity organized and operated principally for the purpose of exporting goods and services, or of providing export-related services to other companies. The Export Trading Company Act of 1982 exempts authorized trading companies from certain provisions of U.S. anti-trust laws.

Extra-territoriality The application of national laws, policies, and practices beyond national boundaries. The United States practices the extra-territorial application of its laws in the area of anti-trust and strategic export controls through its influence over the head offices of U.S.-owned multinational enterprises.

Fast-track Procedures Legislative procedures set forth in Section 151 of the Trade Act of 1974, stipulating that once the President formally submits to Congress a bill implementing an agreement (negotiated under the Act's authority) concerning non-tariff barriers to trade, both Houses must vote on the bill within 90 legislative days. No amendments are permitted. The purpose of these procedures is to assure foreign governments that Congress will act expeditiously on international trade agreements they negotiate with the U.S. government. Under current law, authority to utilize the fast-track procedures expired on 3 January 1988. As the Canada-U.S. FTA was signed on January 2, the fast-track procedure will be used to implement the FTA into U.S. law.

Foreign Exchange Controls Limitations or restrictions on the use of certain types of currency, bank drafts, or other means of payment in order to regulate imports, exports, and the balance of payments.

Foreign Investment Review Agency (FIRA) Agency established by the Canadian federal government in 1974 to monitor and screen foreign direct investment with a view to ensuring that such investment would be of significant benefit to Canada. Its work created major difficulties in Canada-U.S. relations and it was disliked by the business community. It was replaced in 1984 by Investment Canada which has a mandate to attract foreign direct investment to Canada.

Free Trade An economic concept, used for analytical purposes, to denote trade unfettered by government-imposed trade restrictions; also used as a general term to denote the end result of a process of trade liberalization. Freer trade is the comparative term used to denote circumstances between current practice and the achievement of free trade.

Free Trade Area A cooperative arrangement, recognized and authorized under Article XXIV of the GATT, among two or more countries that agree to remove substantially all tariff and non-tariff barriers to trade with each other, while each maintains its own schedule of tariffs and customs measures vis-à-vis all other nations.

Free Trade Zone An area within a country (a seaport, airport, warehouse or any designated area) regarded as being outside its customs territory. Importers may therefore bring goods of foreign origin into such an area without paying customs duties and taxes, pending their eventual processing, transshipment or re-exportation. Free trade zones were numerous and prosperous during an earlier period when tariffs were high. Some still exist in capital cities, transport junctions and major seaports, but their number and prominence have declined as tariffs have been reduced in recent years. Free trade zones are also be known as "free ports", "free warehouses", and "foreign trade zones".

GATT The General Agreement on Tariffs and Trade ("GATT") is a multilateral treaty, subscribed to by 96 countries which together account for more than four-fifths of world trade, delineating rules for international trade. The primary objective of the GATT is to liberalize world trade and place it on a secure basis, thereby contributing to global economic growth and development.

Generalized System of Preferences (GSP) A concept developed within UNCTAD to encourage the expansion of manufactured and semi-manufactured exports from developing countries by making those goods more competitive in developed country markets through tariff preferences. The GSP reflects an international agreement, negotiated at UNCTAD II in New Delhi in 1968, that a temporary and non-reciprocal grant of preferences by developed countries to developing countries would be equitable and, in the long term, mutually beneficial.

GNP Gross National Product.

Government Procurement Purchases of goods by official government agencies. As a non-tariff barrier to trade, it refers to discriminatory purchases from domestic suppliers, even when imported goods are more competitive. See also Buy-National.

Government Procurement Code A code of conduct negotiated under the auspices of the GATT during the Tokyo Round of the MTN that established substantive qualification and procedural standards for tendering and awarding of government contracts for certain Code-covered federal government departments and agencies.

Grandfather Clause A GATT or FTA provision that allows the original signatories to accept an international trade agreement's obligations despite the fact that some existing domestic legislation is otherwise inconsistent with the agreement's provisions. See the GATT Protocol of Provisional Accession and Residual Restrictions. More generally, any clause in an international trade agreement which provides that existing programs, practices and policies are exempt from an obligation is a grandfather clause.

Harmonized Commodity Coding and Description System (HS) A system for classifying goods for customs purposes, formerly known as the Brussels Tariff Nomenclature. Canada adopted the HS as its system for customs classification effective January 1, 1988. The United States is expected to adopt it early in 1988. The HS forms the basis for tariff reductions and rules of origin under the Canada-U.S. FTA.

IBRD (World Bank) International Bank for Reconstruction and Development established, together with the International Monetary Fund, after the Bretton Woods Conference in 1944. Its purpose was to help countries to reconstruct their economies after the damage inflicted by the war. It is prepared to assist member countries by lending to governmental agencies or by guaranteeing private loans. Loans are usually made for fifteen to twenty years and are available to finance agricultural modernization, hydroelectric schemes, port improvement, or general programs of economic reconstruction. The funds come from the developed countries and the World Bank acts as a medium-term loan agency in channeling them to the less developed countries.

IMF International Monetary Fund, established at Bretton Woods in 1944. Its purpose is to restore and promote monetary and economic stability. Its headquarters are in Washington. All OECD and most developing countries are members.

Import Policy Encompasses traditional government policies intended to provide a favorable economic climate for the development of industry in general or specific industrial sectors. Instruments of industrial policy may include tax incentives to promote investments or exports, direct or indirect subsidies, special financing arrangements, protection against foreign competition, worker training programs, regional development programs, assistance for research and development, and measures to assist small business. Historically, the term industrial policy has been associated with at least some degree of centralized economic planning or indicative planning, but this connotation is not always intended by its contemporary advocates.

Import Substitution   An attempt by a country to reduce imports, and hence foreign exchange expenditures, by encouraging the development of domestic industries.

Import Quota   See Quantitative Restriction.

Industrial Policy   Governmental actions affecting, or seeking to affect, the sectoral composition of the economy by influencing the development of particular industries.

Industrial Targeting   The selection by a government, of industries important to the next stage of the nation's economy, and encouragement of their development through explicit policy measures. A frequent goal of such targeting is competitiveness in export markets.

Infant Industry Argument   The view that "temporary protection" for a new industry or firm in a particular country through tariff and non-tariff barriers to imports can help it to become established and eventually competitive in world markets. Historically, new industries that are soundly based and efficiently operated have experienced declining costs as output expands and production experience is acquired. However, industries that have been established and operated with heavy dependence on direct or indirect government subsidies have sometimes found it difficult to relinquish that support. The rationale underlying the Generalized System of Preferences is comparable to that of the infant industry argument.

Injury   The term used in international commerce to describe the effect on domestic producers of a decline in output, lost sales, decline in market share, reduced profits and return on investment, reduced capacity utilization, etc., as a result of import competition. A distinction is often made between "serious" injury (required for emergency safeguards measures) and "material" injury (required for antidumping and countervailing duties).

The requirement, under GATT, that an industry seeking trade relief establish that it has been hurt by foreign competition. In the United States, a finding of injury has always been required for escape clause relief, and since 1979 for the bulk of countervailing duty and antidumping cases as well.

Intellectual Property   A collective term used to refer to original ideas, inventions, designs, writings, films, etc., and protected by copyright, patents, trademarks, and other intellectual property laws.

International Joint Commission Bilateral Canada-U.S. agency responsible for investigating complaints relating to the flow of boundary waters and recommending remedial action. It is often cited as model for dispute resolution in the trade area.

International Trade Commission (ITC) See U.S. International Trade Commission.

Investment Canada See FIRA.

Investment Performance Requirements Special conditions imposed on foreign direct investment by recipient governments, sometimes requiring commitments by prospective investors to export a certain percentage of output, to purchase certain supplies locally, or to ensure the employment of a specified percentage of local labour and management.

Invisibles Trade Items such as freight, insurance, and financial services that are included in a country's balance of payments accounts (in the "current" account), even though they are not recorded as physically visible exports or imports.

ISAC Industry Sector Advisory Committee. Sectoral business advisory committee to the U.S. government during trade negotiations. See also ACTN. Equivalent to Canadian SAGIT.

ITA International Trade Administration of the U.S. Department of Commerce, the branch of government responsible for antidumping and countervailing duty investigations under U.S. trade law. Once the ITA establishes the existence of dumping or subsidization, the ITC determines whether or not there is injury.

ITAC International Trade Advisory Committee. A committee of 33 private sector leaders that advises the Canadian government on trade negotiations, bilateral and multilateral, and other trade-related issues. See also SAGIT.

ITO International Trade Organization, the still-born organization that was to do for trade what the IMF has done for the management of international monetary issues. GATT, the commercial policy chapter of the Havana Charter of the ITO, has gradually gained organizational status and now performs this function.

Kennedy Round The sixth in a series of GATT multilateral trade negotiations.

Kyoto Convention The major international agreement covering customs procedures. It is administered by the Customs Cooperation Council in Brussels, and under its auspices, international specialists yearly add to international standardization of customs procedures by adding protocols and annexes to the Convention.

Least Developed Countries (LDC's)   Some 36 of the world's poorest countries, considered by the United Nations to be the least developed of the less developed countries. Most of them are small in terms of area and population, and some are land-locked or small island countries. They are generally characterized by low per capita incomes, literacy levels, and medical standards; subsistence agriculture; and a lack of exploitable minerals and competitive industries. Many suffer from aridity, floods, hurricanes, and excessive animal and plant pests, and most are situated in the zone 10 to 30 degrees north latitude. These countries have little prospect of rapid economic development in the foreseeable future and are likely to remain heavily dependent upon official development assistance for many years. Most are in Africa, but a few, such as Bangladesh, Afghanistan, Laos, and Nepal, are in Asia. Haiti is the only country in the Western Hemisphere classified by the United Nations as "least developed". See developing countries.

Liberalization   Reductions in tariff and other government measures that restrict world trade, unilaterally, bilaterally or multilaterally. Trade liberalization has been the objective of all GATT trade negotiations.

Market Access   Availability of a national market to products and services from exporting countries, i.e., a government's willingness to permit imports to compete relatively unimpeded with similar domestically-produced goods or services.

Market Disruption   Situation existing when a surge of imports of a given product causes sales of domestically-produced goods to decline to an extent that domestic producers and their employees suffer major economic dislocation.

Mercantilism   A prominent economic philosophy in the 16th and 17th centuries that equated the accumulation and possession of gold and other international monetary assets, such as foreign currency reserves, with national wealth. Although this point of view is generally discredited among 20th century economists and trade policy experts, some contemporary politicians still favour policies designed to create trade "surpluses", such as import substitution and tariff protection for domestic industries, as essential to national economic strength.

Most-Favoured-Nation Treatment (MFN) A commitment that a country will extend to another country the lowest tariff rates it applies to any third country. The MFN principle has been the foundation of the world trading system since the end of World War II. All Contracting Parties to GATT are required to apply MFN treatment to one another under Article I of GATT. Exceptions to this fundamental rule are allowed in the formation of regional trading arrangements, such as free trade areas, provided certain strict criteria are met. See also national treatment.

MTN See Multilateral Trade Negotiations.

Multi-Fibre Arrangement regarding Trade in Textiles (MFA) An international compact under GATT that allows an importing signatory country to apply quantitative restrictions on textiles when it considers them necessary to prevent market disruption. The MFA provides a framework for regulating international trade in textiles and apparel with the objectives of achieving "orderly marketing" of such products, and of avoiding "market disruption" in import countries. It provides a basis on which major importers, such as the United States and the European Community, may negotiate bilateral agreements or, if necessary, impose restraints on imports from low-wage producing countries. It provides, among other things, standards for determining market disruption, minimum levels of import restraints, and annual growth of imports. Since an importing country may impose such quotas unilaterally to restrict rapidly rising textiles imports, many important textile-exporting countries consider it advantageous to enter into bilateral agreements with the principal textile-importing countries. The MFA went into effect of January 1, 1974, was renewed in December 1977, in December 1981, and again in July 1986, for five years. It succeeded the Long-term Agreement on International Trade in Cotton Textiles (the "LTA") which had been in effect since 1962. Whereas the LTA applied only to cotton textiles, the MFA now applies to wool, man-made (synthetic) fiber, silk blend and other vegetable fiber textiles and apparel.

Multilateral Agreement An international trade compact involving three or more parties. For example, the GATT has been, since its establishment in 1947, seeking to promote trade liberalization through multilateral negotiations.

Multilateral Trade Negotiations (MTN) Seven rounds of "Multilateral Trade Negotiations" have been held under the auspices of the GATT since 1947. Each round represented a discrete and lengthy series of interacting bargaining sessions among the participating Contracting Parties in search of mutually beneficial agreements looking toward the reduction of barriers to world trade. The agreements ultimately reached at the conclusion of each round became the new GATT commitments and were important steps in the evolution of the world trading system.

National Treatment   GATT, Article III, provides that a Contracting Party must extend to goods imported from another Contracting Party treatment no less favourable than that accorded to domestic goods with respect to internal taxes, laws, regulations and requirements.

NEP   National Energy Program. Program adopted by the Canadian federal government in 1979 to increase Canadian control and ownership of the energy industry and stimulate exploration and exploitation of Canada's energy resources in a planned and coherent manner. Its more nationalistic elements strained Canada-U.S. relations and, together with FIRA, stood as symbols of Canadian economic nationalism. Many of its more objectionable principles were withdrawn in 1985-86.

Newly Industrializing Countries (NIC's)   Advanced developing countries whose industrial production and exports have grown rapidly in recent years. Examples include Brazil, Hong Kong, Korea, Mexico, Singapore, and Taiwan.

Non-Market Economy   A national economy or a country in which the government seeks to determine economic activity largely through a mechanism of central planning, as in the Soviet Union, in contrast to a market economy that depends heavily upon market forces to allocate productive resources. In a "non-market" economy, production targets, prices, costs, investment allocations, raw materials, labour, international trade, and most other economic aggregates are manipulated within a national economic plan drawn up by a central planning authority, and hence the public sector makes the major decisions affecting demand and supply within the national economy. See also State-Trading Countries.

Non-Tariff Barriers (NTB's)   Government measures or policies other than tariffs which restrict or distort international trade. Examples include import quotas, discriminatory government procurement practices, and discriminatory product standards. Such measures have become more conspicuous impediments to trade as tariffs have been reduced as a result of successive GATT rounds.

OECD Organization for Economic Cooperation and Development. Paris-based organization of industrialized countries responsible for study and cooperation of a broad range of economic, trade, scientific and educational issues. Membership includes U.S., Canada, Japan, Australia, New Zealand, France, Italy, Belgium, Germany (FR), Netherlands, Luxembourg, Denmark, UK, Ireland, Greece, Spain, Portugal, Austria, Switzerland, Finland, Iceland, Norway, Sweden, Turkey and Yugoslavia.

OPEC Organization of Petroleum Exporting Countries

Orderly Marketing Agreements (OMA's) International agreements negotiated between two or more governments, in which the trading partners agree to restrain the growth of trade in specified "sensitive" products, usually through the imposition of import quotas. Orderly Marketing Agreements are intended to ensure that future trade increases will not disrupt, threaten or impair competitive industries or their workers in importing countries.

Panel of Experts Subgroups of the GATT or the FTA established by the Contracting Parties or member countries on an ad hoc basis to study a particular facet of GATT work. Panels are generally composed of three to five persons who serve in their individual capacity, acting not as representatives of nations, but as experts or objective judges of particular matters.

Par Value The official fixed exchange rate between two currencies or between a currency and a specific weight of gold or a basket of currencies.

Phasing See transitional measures.

Principal Supplier The country that is the most important source of a particular product imported by another country. In negotiations conducted under the GATT, a country offering to reduce import duties or other barriers on a particular item generally expects the principal supplier of the imported item to offer, in exchange, to reduce restrictions on an item. Both countries then automatically grant the same concessions to all other countries to which they have agreed to accord most-favored-nation treatment, including all Contracting Parties to GATT. See also Most-Favoured-Nation Treatment and Reciprocity.

Product Standards As defined by the Agreement on Technical Barriers to Trade (Product Standards Code), a product standard or a technical regulation specifies certain required characteristics of a product such as quality, performance, safety, or dimensions. It may include terminology, symbols, testing and test methods, packaging, marking, or labelling requirements as they apply to a product.

Protectionism   The deliberate use or encouragement of restrictions on imports to enable relatively inefficient domestic producers to compete successfully with foreign producers.

Quantitative Restrictions (QR's)   Explicit limits or quotas, on the amounts of particular commodities that can be imported or exported during a specified time period, usually measured by volume but sometimes by value. A quota may be applied on a "selective" basis, with varying limits set according to the country of origin, or on a quantitative global basis that specifies only the total limit and thus tends to benefit more efficient suppliers. Quotas are frequently administered through a system of licensing. GATT Article XI generally prohibits the use of quantitative restrictions, except under conditions specified by other GATT articles; Article XIX permits quotas to safeguard certain industries from damage by rapidly rising imports; Article XII and Article XVIII provide that quotas may be imposed for balance of payments reasons under circumstances laid out in Article XV; Article XX permits special measures to apply to public health, gold stocks, items of archeological or historic interest and several other categories of goods; and Article XXI recognizes the overriding importance of national security. Article XII provides that quantitative restrictions, whenever applied, should be non-discriminatory.

Quebec Declaration   Statement of political intent adopted by Prime Minister Brian Mulroney and President Ronald Reagan at Quebec City, March 18, 1985, providing for formal exploration of a free-trade agreement covering trade in goods and services.

Quota   A limit of the quantity of a product that may be imported by (or sold to) a country. Import quotas are enforced by the importing nation, export quotas by the country of origin.

Reciprocal Trade Agreements Act of 1934   The law which provided authority for the U.S. government to enter into bilateral agreements for reciprocal tariff reductions. Through successive extensions and amendments, it also authorized U.S. participation in the first five GATT Rounds of multilateral trade negotiations. It was superseded by the Trade Expansion Act of 1962.

Reciprocity   The practice by which governments extend similar concessions to each other, as when one government lowers its tariffs or other barriers impeding its imports in exchange for equivalent concessions from a trading partner on barriers affecting its exports (a "balance of concessions"). Reciprocity has traditionally been a principal objective of negotiators in GATT "rounds". Reciprocity is also defined as "mutuality of benefits", "quid pro quo", and "equivalence" of "advantages". GATT Part IV (especially GATT Article XXXVI) and the "Enabling Clause" of the Tokyo Round "Framework Agreement" exempt developing countries from the rigorous application of reciprocity in their negotiations with developed countries.

Reciprocity Agreement   Historical term referring to trade agreements between Canada and the United States providing for reciprocal trade concessions, including the 1854 Elgin-Marcy Treaty and the aborted 1911 agreement.

Residual Restrictions   Quantitative restrictions that have been maintained by governments before they became Contracting Parties to GATT and, hence, permissible under the GATT "grandfather clause". Most of the residual restrictions still in effect are maintained by developed countries against the imports of agricultural products. See also Grandfather Clause, and Quantitative Restrictions.

Retaliation   Action taken by a country to restrain imports from a country that has increased a tariff or imposed other measures that adversely affect the first country's exports in a manner inconsistent with GATT. The GATT, in certain circumstances, permits such reprisal, although this has very rarely been practiced. The value of trade affected by such retaliatory measures should, in theory, approximately equal the value affected by the initial import restriction.

Reverse Preferences   Tariff advantages once offered by developing countries to imports from certain developed countries that granted them preferences. Reverse preferences characterized trading arrangements between the European Community and some developing countries prior to the advent of the Generalized System of Preferences (GSP) and the signing of the Lomé Convention. See European Community, Generalized System of Preferences.

Round of Trade   A cycle of multilateral trade negotiations under the aegis of GATT, culminating in simultaneous trade agreements among participating countries to reduce tariff and non-tariff barriers to trade. Seven "rounds" have been completed thus far: Geneva, 1947-48; Annecy, France, 1949; Torquay, England, 1950-51; Geneva, 1956; Geneva, 1960-62 (the Dillon Round); Geneva, 1963-67 (the Kennedy Round); and Geneva, 1973-79 (the Tokyo Round). A new round, the Uruguay Round, started in September 1986.

Rules of Origin The term for the set of measures used to differentiate between goods originating in one country from those in another for the purpose of application of trade measures such as tariffs. Such rules are very important for countries which are members of a free-trade area to ensure that only goods originating in one or all of the member countries will receive preferential tariff treatment.

Safeguards The term "safeguards" refers to emergency actions in the form of additional duties or import quotas applied to fairly traded imports which cause or threaten serious injury to domestic producers. The imposition of such measures is permitted under Article XIX of the GATT.

SAGIT Sectoral Advisory Group on International Trade. Fifteen such groups have been established to provide the Canadian federal government with advice on trade negotiations and trade-related matters from a sectoral perspective. See also ITAC.

Section 201 (Trade Act of 1974) U.S. escape clause, safeguards or emergency action law designed to implement Article XIX of the GATT. It allows the President to impose measures, such as duties or quantitative restrictions, where a sudden increase in imports is causing or threatening to cause serious injury to a domestic industry. Canada has similar legislation in section 8 of the Customs Tariff and section 5 of the Export and Import Permits Act. See Escape Clause and Safeguards.

Section 301 (Trade Act of 1974) Provision of U.S. law that enables the President to withdraw concessions or restrict imports from countries that discriminate against U.S. exports, subsidize their own exports to the United States, or engage in other unjustifiable or unreasonable practices that burden or discriminate against U.S. trade. Canada has similar legislation in the Customs Tariff, section 7.

Services Economic activities the result of which is the provision of services rather than goods. Includes such diverse activities as transportation, communications, insurance, banking, advertising, consulting, distribution, engineering, medicine, education, etc. It is the fastest growing area of economic activity in Canada. Two-thirds of working Canadians are now employed in the service sector. Trade in services takes place when a service is exported from a supplier nation to another nation, such as an international airflight, the extension of credit, or the design of a bridge.

Smoot-Hawley (Tariff Act of 1930)   U.S. protectionist legislation that raised tariff rates on most articles imported by the United States, triggering comparable tariff increases by U.S. trading partners. The Tariff Act of 1930 is also known as the Smoot-Hawley Act. Many of its non-tariff provisions, e.g., those pertaining to anti-dumping or countervailing duties, remain the U.S. law today, either in its original form or as amended.

Special Drawing Rights (SDR's)   Created in 1969 by the IMF as a supplemental international monetary reserve asset. SDR's are available to governments through the IMF and may be used in transactions between the IMF and member governments. IMF member countries have agreed to regard SDR's as complementary to gold and reserve currencies in settling their international accounts. The union value of an SDR reflects the foreign exchange value of a "basket" of currencies of several major trading countries (the U.S. dollar, the German mark, the French franc, the Japanese yen, the British pound). The SDR has become the unit of account used by the IMF and several national currencies are pegged to it. Some commercial banks accept deposits denominated in SDR's (although they are unofficial and not the same units transacted among governments and the IMF).

Special Import Measures Act (SIMA)   Canadian legislation adopted in 1984 following four years of study and debate incorporating Canadian rights and obligations flowing from the Tokyo Round of GATT negotiations in the area of antidumping and countervailing duties. It provides for basically similar procedures for antidumping and countervailing investigations including separate inquiries into the existence of dumping or subsidization and their margin by the Department of National Revenue, and of material injury by the Canadian Import Tribunal.

Specific Duty or Tariff   An import tax set at a fixed amount per unit or per unit of measure regardless of the value of the item imported. For comparison, see Ad Valorem Tariff.

Subsidies Code   A code of conduct negotiated under the auspices of GATT during the Tokyo Round of the MTN that expanded on Article VI by establishing both substantive and procedural standards for domestic countervailing duty proceedings as well as multilateral obligations regarding notification and dispute settlement in the area of subsidy practices. See also Code of Conduct and Subsidy.

Subsidy   An economic or financial benefit granted by a government to producers of goods often to strengthen their competitive position. The subsidy may be direct (e.g. a cash grant) or indirect (e.g. low-interest export credits guaranteed by a government agency). Not all "subsidies" are "countervailable." See Countervailing Duties.

Surcharge or surtax   A tariff or tax on imports in addition to the existing tariff; may be imposed as a safeguards measure under the Canadian Customs Tariff. See Emergency Action, Safeguards.

Tariff   A duty (or tax) levied upon goods imported from one customs area into another. Tariffs raise the prices of imported goods, thus making them less competitive within the market of the importing country. After seven "rounds" of GATT trade negotiations that focused mainly on tariff reductions, tariffs are less important measures of protection than they used to be. The term "tariff" often refers to a comprehensive list or "schedule" of merchandise specifying the rate of duty to be paid to the government for importing products listed. The tariff rate is the rate at which imported goods are taxed.

Tariff Act of 1930   U.S. trade legislation, also known as the Smoot-Hawley Tariff Act which, as amended, provides the basic trade law of the United States, particularly with respect to antidumping and countervailing duties. Its tariff provisions raised the U.S. tariff to unprecedented levels and contributed to the Great Depression of the 1930s. Smoot-Hawley became synonymous with the Beggar-Thy-Neighbor policies of that period.

Tariff Escalation   A situation in which tariffs on manufactured goods are relatively high, tariffs on semi-processed goods are moderate, and tariffs on raw materials are nonexistent or very low. "Escalation", which exists in the tariff schedules of most developed countries, is said to discourage the development of manufacturing industries in resource rich countries.

Tariff Schedule   A comprehensive list of goods by tariff classification, specifying categories of goods and the tariffs rate applicable to such goods, depending upon their country of origin. See Harmonized System, Tariff.

Terms of Trade   The volume of exports that can be traded for a given volume of imports. Changes in the terms of trade are generally measured by comparing changes in the ratio of export prices to import prices. The terms of trade are considered to have improved when a given volume of exports can be exchanged for a larger volume of imports. Some economists have discerned an overall deteriorating trend in this ratio for developing countries as a whole. Other economists maintain that whereas the terms of trade may have become less favourable for specific countries during certain periods, and even for all developing countries during some periods, the same terms of trade have improved for other developing countries in the same periods and perhaps for most developing countries during other periods.

TNO Trade Negotiations Office. The special office established by the government of Canada in 1985 to prepare for and conduct bilateral trade negotiations with the United States as well as multilateral trade negotiations.

Tokyo Round Seventh in a series of multilateral trade negotiations held under the auspices of GATT, launched in Tokyo in 1973 and concluded in 1979. Several Codes, including the Subsidies Code and the Antidumping Code, resulted from this round.

Trade Act of 1974 U.S. legislation signed into law on 3 January 1975, which granted the President authority to enter the Tokyo Round and negotiate international agreements to reduce tariffs and non-tariff barriers. (See also Fast-Track Procedures.) The Act also amended U.S. law governing the escape clause, antidumping, and countervailing duties; expanded trade adjustment assistance; established guidelines for granting MFN status to Eastern bloc states; and granted limited trade preferences (GSP) to less developed countries.

Trade Agreements Act of 1979 U.S. legislation which approved and implemented the trade agreements or "Codes" negotiated during the Tokyo Round. It made U.S. law consistent with the Tokyo Round Codes, and substantially revised the countervailing duty and antidumping laws, extended the President's authority to negotiate non-tariff barrier agreements, and required the President to reorganize Executive Branch trade functions.

Trade Expansion Act of 1962 U.S. legislation authorizing U.S. participation in the Kennedy Round of multilateral trade negotiations, which also amended the escape clause procedures and established the Trade Adjustment Assistance (TAA) program.

Trade Diversion A shift in the sourcing of imports that occurs as a result of altering a country's import policies or practices. For example, the establishment of a customs union will cause countries participating in the new economic unit to import goods from other countries in the union that previously were imported from countries outside the union. According to some trade theorists, if the "trade creation" resulting from the customs union, that is, the new trade taking place that would not have taken place otherwise exceeds the trade diversion, the customs union will improve consumer welfare and will entail a more efficient allocation of resources.

Trade Liberalization A general term used to denote the gradual process of removing tariff and non-tariff barriers. Seven rounds of negotiations under GATT, since 1947, have resulted in a large measure of trade liberalization among industrialized countries.

Trade and Tariff Act of 1984 U.S. trade legislation which extended the President's authority to grant trade preferences, authorized the negotiation of a free trade agreement with Israel, amended the antidumping and countervailing duty laws, and provided authority to enforce export restraint agreements on steel.

Transfer of Technology The movement of modern or scientific methods of production or distribution from one enterprise, institution or country to another, as through foreign investment, international trade licensing of patent rights, technical assistance or training.

Transitional Measures Those measures in place for a limited period of time during which a new trade agreement is gradually implemented. The Tokyo Round tariff reductions, for example, are being phased in over a period of eight years. Other transitional measures could include, for example, the right to take certain temporary emergency action measures or the right in the FTA to establish a binational panel to review a final antidumping or ·countervailing duty order.

Transparency Visibility and clarity of laws, regulations and government practices. Some of the Codes of Conduct negotiated during the Tokyo Round sought to increase the transparency of non-tariff barriers by requiring countries to notify and consult with each other about measures that may affect trade and to publish their government's decisions. (See Product Standards Code, Government Procurement Code.)

Trigger Price Mechanism (TPM) A system, developed and enforced during the Carter administration, of restraining steel imports by monitoring them for possible dumping. Under the TPM, an antidumping investigation was to be "triggered" if the price of an imported steel product fell below the production costs of the world's most efficient producer of that product.

UNCTAD   United Nations Conference on Trade and Development. A quasi-autonomous body within the United Nations system, intended to focus special attention on measures that might be taken to accelerate the pace of economic development in the developing countries. The conference was first convened in Geneva in 1964, and has met quadrennially since that date.

Unfair Trade   A term used to describe trade in dumped, subsidized or counterfeit goods; the use of the term has steadily widened as U.S. trade remedy laws have defined new practices that are considered to harm the export and import interests of U.S. companies.

Uruguay Round   Eighth in a series of multilateral trade negotiations held under the auspices of GATT. This round was launched at Punta del Este, Uruguay in September, 1986. Subjects in this round include agriculture, subsidies, trade in services, trade-related investment, safeguards, intellectual property, and dispute settlement. Negotiators are working toward an "early harvest" at the GATT mid-term review late in 1988.

USITC   U.S. International Trade Commission. An independent U.S. fact-finding and regulatory agency whose members make determinations of injury and recommendations for relief in antidumping, countervailing duty and Section 201 cases. In addition, upon the request of Congress or the President, or on its own initiative, the Commission conducts comprehensive studies of specific industries and trade problems, and the probable impact on specific U.S. industries of proposed reductions in U.S. tariffs and non-tariff trade barriers. The USITC was created by the Trade Act of 1974 as the successor agency to the U.S. Tariff Commission, which was created in 1916.

USTR   United States Trade Representative. A Minister in the Executive Office of the President, with cabinet-level and ambassadorial rank, charged with advising the President and leading and coordinating the U.S. government position in international trade negotiations and the development of trade policy. (USTR also designates the White House office which the Representative heads). Established by the Carter administration in 1980, USTR succeeded the position of Special Trade Representative (STR), which was created in the Trade Expansion Act of 1962, and whose status and authority was strengthened in the Trade Act of 1974.

Valuation The appraisal of the value of imported goods by customs officials for the purpose of determining the amount of duty payable in the importing country. The GATT Customs Valuation Code obligates signatory governments to use the "transaction value" of imported goods, or the price actually paid or payable for them, as the principal basis for valuing the goods for customs purposes.

Value-Added Tax (VAT) An indirect tax on consumption that is levied at each discrete point in the chain of production and distribution, from the raw material stage to final consumption. Each processor or merchant pays a tax proportional to the amount by which he increases the value of the goods he purchases for resale after making his own contribution. The Value-Added Tax is imposed throughout the European Community and EFTA countries, but the tax rates have not been harmonized among those countries.

Variable Levy A tariff subject to alterations as world market prices change, the alterations being designed to assure that the import price after payment of duty will equal a predetermined "gate" price. The variable levy of the European Community, the best known example, equals the difference between the target price for domestic agricultural producers and lowest offers for imported commodities on a C.I.F. basis. The amount of the levy is adjusted daily for changes in the world market situation in the case of grains, fortnightly for dairy products, and quarterly for pork.

Voluntary Restraint Agreements (VRA's); Voluntary Export Restraints (VER's) Informal arrangements through which exporters voluntarily agree to restrain certain exports, usually through export quotas, to avoid economic dislocation in an ·importing country, and to avert the possible imposition of import restrictions by the importing country. Such arrangements do not normally entail "compensation" for the exporting country, and are negotiated outside of the GATT.

WIPO World Intellectual Property Organization

Working Party A type of GATT or FTA subgroup established by the GATT Council or the Canada-U.S. Trade Commission on an *ad hoc* basis to study a particular facet of its work and to make proposals for future reforms. Customarily, membership in a Working Party is specified on the basis of nationality with each country determining which individual(s) will participate. Upon completion of their studies, Working Parties report back to the member countries, the Council or the Commission and may make recommendations on possible courses of action.

Index